DREAM PALACE

DREAM PALACE

HERBERT MORRIS

1817

Harper & Row, Publishers, New York
Cambridge, Philadelphia, San Francisco, London
Mexico City, São Paulo, Singapore, Sydney

Some of the poems in this collection originally appeared in *The New Criterion, The Paris Review, Poetry, Salmagundi,* and *Shenandoah.*

Grateful acknowledgment is made for permission to reprint the excerpt from "From the Cupola" in *Nights and Days* by James Merrill. Copyright © 1966 by James Merrill. Reprinted with the permission of Atheneum Publishers, Inc., and Chatto & Windus.

FIRST EDITION

Designer: C. Linda Dingler

Library of Congress Cataloging-in-Publication Data

Morris, Herbert, date
   Dream palace.

   I. Title.
PS3563.087434D7   1986   811'.54   85-45217
ISBN 0-06-015536-1   86 87 88 89 90 HC 10 9 8 7 6 5 4 3 2 1
ISBN 0-06-096008-6 (pbk.)   86 87 88 89 90 HC 10 9 8 7 6 5 4 3 2 1

For James Merrill

*"that dream whose arrows pierced
us through and through"*

Contents

My Parents on Their Honeymoon: A Snapshot

They would be boating that day on the lake,
though there is not a spinnaker in sight
whose full-blown white-on-white would no doubt blind you
if the picture depicted prows and sails.

All one has is this landing, this bleached dock,
its planks laid plank by plank, symmetrically,
the boards nailed parallel to sky and water,
in the middle of which a single bench,

forlorn in that expanse, disconsolate,
has been positioned, almost like a stage prop,
the sky immense, the water's width no less so,
the silence rising from the woods resounding.

Water stretches from here to the horizon.
If one were to set out early one morning
and, all day, all day, tack south in the sun,
one would still not reach the far shore by nightfall.

This morning they have stepped from the hotel,
though nothing that resembles a hotel,
nothing whatever, has revealed itself.
That it stood in these woods, just left or right

of the view finder, or on some low slope
whose scope so small a lens might not encompass;
that the gold roof tiles glittered in the sun,
setting the trees ablaze; that five verandas,

sweeping down to the lakeshore in grand style,
yielded five unobstructed views of water,
offered a night breeze laced with salt and pine;
that the sumptuous, hand-sewn, French silk sheets

were to be turned back late that night, late each night,
and the down pillows propped, in preparation
for that marvelous traffic whose procession
of dreamers, visionaries, voyagers,

just-married couples, would lie here together,
deeply, tenderly, briefly, then move on;
that the kitchen, that moment, was preparing
a spiced sauce to be served at lunch that day

(the boating party just launched, under way,
or on the verge of getting under way,
the sun high, climbing higher, the wind right,
the day clear, flawless, all the signs auspicious),

a demi-glace not too bland, not too dark,
to spark the appetites of those young couples
holding hands at side tables seating two,
must be taken on faith, wholly on faith.

My father lies full-length on a small bench
too short, too wooden, to provide much comfort,
too factual, perhaps, to let him doze.
Its slats weave a vague fretwork with the sun.

He wears a long-sleeved shirt with narrow stripes
through which one sees the wind, that moment, passing,
the perfect shirt, it seems now, for the sail,
and on his head a small, felt racing beanie

young grooms may well have sported at the lake
that summer, though the camera fails to find them,

finds only my father benched at the landing,
alone with sky, woods, fretwork, light, wind, water.

My father, lying face up, takes the sun,
my mother nowhere visible, of course,
since it is she who handles the box camera,
who, for the future (this is how we looked,

this, by implication, is who we were;
will it be far from 1921
to those others, years later, we become?),
must want this picture of him for herself,

random, off-guard, unposed, relaxed, eyes closed,
My Young Husband in His Silk Sailing Shirt
with Narrow Stripes and Long Sleeves, and a Beanie
Signifying We Are About to Sail,

though she may be unsure those words are apt,
doubtful her caption will do this scene justice,
unversed as to what cameras can do,
cannot do, what one should expect them to do,

not certain what the lake is, or the woods,
why the silence persists in rising from them,
where, if a hotel stands, the hotel stands,
magical, dim, cool, shimmering, dream palace,

what today's sky means, may mean, where one starts,
where one ends (lake, woods, hotel, sky, self, husband),
given this seamless world (June, '21)
whose separations have yet to appear,

have yet to make themselves apparent to her
(my mother is nineteen: there will be time).
Without even her shadow to intrude,
her presence, too, her weight, one takes on faith.

3

Eyes closed, my father dreams of embarkation,
of landfall, of this slender, brown-eyed bride
with such rich, long, dark hair, such fine, pale ankles,
sensing her circling somewhere to the rear,

somewhere between himself and sky, woods, water,
prowling and searching for some perfect moment,
some perfect stance, before she trips the shutter
in an attempt to fix him for all time there.

The silence that prevailed prevails, persists,
perhaps increases, though one can mistake
the silence, he may think, that is the woods
for the silence, just as vast, that is water.

My father thinks he knows the lake, the woods,
if not quite what they are, what they may be.
Eyes closed, he glimpses, dimly, the hotel,
gold-roofed, silk-sheeted, near and soon, resplendent.

Boardwalk

From what I remember of the light's angle,
of the sun, mornings, hammering our backs,
slamming our shoulders, playing on our faces,
surf on one side, horizon on the other,
we must be walking back to the hotel,
four of us, having, midway, made the turn
marking the farthest south we would advance.
Now we head north once more, the four of us,
Mother and Father at the center, I
next to Mother, my brother flanking Father,
I (even then) the one nearest the sea,
my brother, on the landward side, the farthest.
Mother holds my gloved hand in her gloved hand,
very gently, it seems, encourages me
to smile for the roving photographer
(clusters of them, from seven on each morning,
patrol the boardwalk, one end to the other,
springing from nowhere when a family group
or a honeymoon couple has been sighted)
who has just now, just now, appeared before us,
materializing, it seems, from the sea,
promising a family portrait not merely
true-to-life but, should that be possible,
what might prove infinitely better: truer.
Mother and Father are, in time, persuaded;
they smile, my brother smiles, and I, encouraged
(though perhaps I would have done so regardless),
smile, too, that same half-squint, half-grin I wear now
when the sun slams too hard, or the light's glare

sets much too fierce a blaze, and light pours, pours,
blinding me a little (though it is blindness
I sought, and blindness, even now, I seek).

Father has slipped his arm beneath my brother's,
shyly, perhaps, yet not self-consciously,
a tenderness quite nearly inadvertent,
almost precisely counterbalancing
Mother's gesture in taking my gloved hand,
though Father's movement may be in response
to the sudden appearance of this young man
aiming his black machine at us, promising
something truer than the mere true-to-life:
fidelity, the real made much more so,
life, or four lives, made large as life, or larger,
because of what the lens would have us see—
an idea quite irresistible,
he thinks, to family groups (the four of us),
to young couples spending their honeymoons
watching the moon rise, hearing the waves break,
walking the boardwalk, back, and forth, and back,
until, at last, they turn to their hotels
(turn back, or turn again, or for the first time;
what shall matter is that they make the turn)
at some point farthest south from here, advancing,
and, in the dark, dream splendor in the turn.

Mother's coat, long and black, with a fox collar
from whose recesses her face now looks out,
pale flower framed by rings of jet-black petals,
is fastened with one button at the waist.
With the gloved hand not holding mine, she clutches
a small purse, also black, close to her chest.
Her cloche, black, too, has scallops of thin half-moons
cut delicately to ride on her forehead,
her dark hair visible at the right temple
where the brim of the cloche, seen slowly rising,

has been designed, one gathers, to reveal it.
Her shoes seem somehow splendid, though they seem
wholly unremarkable, too, at first glance,
at second glance, as well: thin, pointed tips
catching the light that showers us that day,
their balance, their proportion, sane and just,
undecorated, plain, above all quiet,
holding beautifully, it seems, to their ground,
Mother's ground, holding neither tentatively
nor tenaciously, leaving room between
for where she stands, or may decide to stand,
the secret lodged within them, should there be one,
Mother's secret, as well: simplicity
(disputably, we are the shoes we wear).

Father, beside her, grey on grey on grey,
wears a grey felt hat, grey trousers, grey spats,
and a form-fitting coat of darker grey.
The hat's brim throws deep shade across his eyes.
He wears a freshly starched shirt collar, white,
and a dark necktie in the center of which
two or three tiny diamonds of a stickpin
snare the light with each step that Father takes.
The hand closer to Mother (Father's right)
holds itself in check where the coat cuff ends,
the thumb gripped by the other fingers, hidden,
secreted in the palm, none of the fingers
extended, pointed down (some vast restraint
seems locked within that small gesture, some sense
of instinctive reserve), almost as though
Father does not yet quite know what to do
with that hand, with the fingers of that hand,
the one I have described as nearest Mother.
Dapper, stylish, meticulously groomed,
light lapping his dark grey, form-fitting coat,
his felt hat tipped at just the proper angle,
spats preserving the high shine on his shoes,

strolling with wife, with two sons, back and forth,
from one end of the boardwalk to the other,
diamonds lighting small fires in his necktie,
nests of shadows clustering in the folds
where, at mid-calf, mid-shin, his trousers break,
Father has the look of someone substantial.

My brother, the most difficult to fathom
(though I by no means claim ease with the others),
is, that winter, past ten, not yet eleven.
What can one say about a boy of ten?
I might describe apparel: his blue coat,
the scarf tucked in the collar, leather gloves.
I might mention his cap, his argyle socks,
the knickers showing from beneath his coat.
What, in any case, would you know of him
you would not know of any boy past ten
brought by his parents to the beach one Friday
for Father's birthday weekend late in winter?
I think my guess is that he would be elsewhere,
given the choice—I cannot say just where
(even strolling the boardwalk that day, he seems
in the process of drifting off, like smoke),
though I should add that nothing in the picture,
nothing I can quite specify, says that.
If the picture were faded, streaked, showed age marks,
edges blistered, deformed, sections bleached out,
some faces—and lives with them—turning yellow,
too late to be retrieved, to be pulled back,
it is my brother I would have expected
to fade, to disappear before the eyes,
to bear whatever loss or devastation
the photograph had visited upon it,
my brother in whom damage would have spread,
in whom the most destruction would occur,
his figure, his, first, foremost, lashed, effaced.
Yet the feeling persists: that smile he smiles,

that look his eyes bear, even that half-shadow
cast by his cap across his brows, his forehead,
are all (and it lies in nothing apparent,
nothing the photographer caught that morning,
salt on the air, the wind up, the surf breaking,
search as I may, pursuing, lead by lead,
each likely, or unlikely, lead, all fruitless,
nothing, nothing whatever, one can hold to,
point to, identify, articulate,
hope to articulate) quite temporary,
wavering, failing, falling, giving way.

The pocket of my brother's coat we see,
the one so sharply outlined by the sun,
bulges with something in it (games? a book?),
lending distortion to his silhouette;
with Father anchoring him to the boardwalk,
with all of us (I could not know it then)
somehow, each in his way, engaged, in secret,
in some last, futile, desperate attempt
to keep him here with us, here in the Thirties,
here on these pine-wood planks skirting the sea,
under light of a morning in late winter
assailing us all day, on all sides, full force,
making us squint, casting shadows, half-shadows,
across our living, not-yet-ravaged faces,
lighting our shoes, our lovely, Thirties shoes,
our spats in flame, our stickpins raging, raging,
our boys' caps, our black cloches, our fedoras,
one wonders what it was stored in that pocket,
what he might have kept in it, chose to keep,
what seemed to him worthy enough for saving,
what (perhaps more than anything) he held to,
however tenuous and brief the holding.

In the photo, his shoes seem new, unscathed,
looking as though they had not yet been walked in,

9

the light that issues from them so contained,
so manageable, it appears, his smile
so compliant, his breathing, like his presence,
so unobtrusive, I am almost certain
(definitiveness quite eludes me here:
freedom from doubt, pertaining to my brother,
is arrogance, mistaken, self-deluding)
the way he holds himself may have to do
with having come to learn—how can I say this?—
what it will be to die, and to die young.

The woolen cap and leather gloves I wear
match the cap and the gloves my brother wears.
A white silk scarf is knotted at my throat.
I am dressed for a cold day: collar turned,
scarf tucked about my neck, brown leather leggings
shielding my legs from the high coastal wind.
I am smiling, of course, and, as reported,
of the four I am closest to the sea,
so that, as we move north, light strikes me first.
I reach only to Mother's waist, am blond.
I squint beneath the sun. My cap is set
at what one wants to call a jaunty angle.
I take short steps that winter; I am four.
The waves assault the coast; I hear the gulls cry.
My breath, turned smoke, is rising on the air.
In the background, not completely in focus,
lies the resort itself (the sea unseen),
a mise-en-scène of small shops, baths, hotels
lining the boardwalk; a few scattered figures,
fading to haze, to blur, loom in the distance,
early walkers like us, although it seems
we have the boardwalk largely to ourselves.
Something about me seems so wholly present,
so here-and-nowhere-else (the way my face
takes light? the confidence I seem to walk with?
how I grip Mother's hand?), it is a struggle

to imagine Father, arm slipped in mine,
taking care to hold me before I drift off,
having to anchor me, needing to root me
here in the Thirties, where one finds oneself,
beneath this clamor February sends up
from one end of the boardwalk to the other,
not fifty paces from where we are strolling
this tumult of grey-blue-green sea, momentous,
unrelenting, asking, over and over,
one question, one, offering just one answer
(neither of which, it seems, has been disclosed,
not that year nor in any season since),
spray on the air beading our lips, our faces.

(Scrutinizing this photograph with me,
decades later, tracking down lost details
until, one by one, each has been recovered,
restored to its incomparable luster,
the past freed from the dust which settles on it,
freed from the past, made whole, retrieved intact—
Those were drop earrings I wore, see them? pearls;
that vast collar was fox, black-as-night fox,
and your leggings had buttons down the side
which I would fasten with a button hook—,
slowly, quite slowly, Mother turns to me—
the turn as lovely as the need to turn—,
tears filling her eyes, spilling to her cheeks,
whispers these words: You two were dazzling, dazzling.)

We must be walking back to the hotel,
having gone as far south as we intended.
There is an Oriental curio shop
in the lobby, beside the elevator,
where, each day, I linger, peer through the glass.
In a window showcase framed with bamboo,
slivers of sun caught among painted fan spokes,
teak elephants, necklaces, cloisonné

butterflies, daggers, jardinières, blue inkpots,
I spy a small, square box of jade and ivory,
its latch whittled of ebony and pearl,
as beautiful as anything, at four,
I have seen, hope to see, remember seeing.
I study butterflies, blue inkpots, daggers,
elephants, but it is this, this small, square box,
I pause at, point to, dream of; I say nothing.
Father and I enter the shop; a bell chimes,
and the proprietor comes from the rear,
partitioned by a screen of sleeping dragons.
The man wears sandals and a silk kimono.
Father says he has the extreme good fortune,
this man, of having on display a box
it would give his son, me, pleasure to hold,
much pleasure, in fact. Is this possible?
The man unlocks the showcase, lifts the box,
places it, gently, gently, in my hand.
There are carvings of nightingales and pine boughs
spilling across its surface, down its sides,
a latticework of intricate cross-weavings
depicting some lost, mythic underbrush
in China (or in paradise)—black loam
(as black as Mother's fox, perhaps), a stream,
a forest floor so dense, so rich, so tangled,
anything, one suspects, will grow here, flourish,
a grove of chinaberry trees to one side,
to the other a stand of one of each:
lime, weeping cherry, almond, plum, quince, peach,
a great, fat, plume-tailed goldfish, in the foreground,
spouting water from jade-encrusted lips.

It is a puzzle as well as a box
(he is addressing me as much as Father):
first the spring which frees the latch must be found
before you can know what may lie inside.
And, should you find it (he now presses something,

and the lid opens), this is the reward
for your perseverance, your cleverness:
a second box, exactly like the first,
nightingales, pine boughs, goldfish, fruit trees, stream,
is nestled in the first, fitting precisely.
But your confidence should not be excessive,
the man says, smiling, showing two gold teeth;
there is a latch to be sought out here, too,
but placed not where the first latch has been placed.
It is altogether another search,
another quest, you might say, to embark on.
His fingers glide across the second box,
smaller than the first; its lid now springs back.
Within it lies a box, quite small, a third box,
nightingales, pine boughs, goldfish clinging to it,
crowding the glossy jade and ivory surface,
not a space left unfilled, undecorated.
Perhaps the third box should remain unopened,
at least for now, he says; when you have left here,
you can take with you dreams of what it holds,
what it may hold, even perhaps imagine
what, as well, it may not hold, for which one must
leave in the mind as much room as one can.
The box may do just that, no more than that:
keep us, for perhaps just a little longer,
open to astonishment, to surprise,
accessible to what one understands
dimly, imperfectly, or not at all,
just awhile longer, no more, just awhile.

We must be walking back to the hotel.
We will ride the elevator to rooms
streaked all day with the sun, fronting the sea.
(Even here, rising, I will hear the waves break.)
Father's gift to me will lie on my bed
nestled in Chinese-red rice paper spattered
with dragonflies and willows in gold leaf.

I will hold it, run my thumb on the inlay,
turn it, glimpse views of paradise (or China),
ivory nightingales perched on jade pine boughs,
a fish standing in midstream spouting silver,
pure silver, from two semi-precious lips,
content, for now, to let the latches wait,
postpone the search, delay that quest of quests
to which the man in sandals had alluded,
at least until some principle is mastered
(vague, though no less substantial for its vagueness)
of where the puzzle ends and box begins,
where the border between them, evenings, lies,
why paradise cannot be China, too,
discrepancies of which I have no inkling.
Father will order cocktails from room service
as the sky darkens; after naps and baths,
we will descend once more to the first level,
a balcony overlooking the lobby
(Palm Terrace, the old operator sings out,
as he slides the door back and we debark).
From our window table we see the first stars,
winter stars, brilliant, distant, ringed with ice.
(I know the phases of the moon, the planets,
names for the constellations, thanks to Father.)
Mother wears a green frock tiered with black fringe
and a choker of beads about her throat
whose stones I ask the name for: opal, opal.
(Each night I ask, loving the music words make;
in the mind the sound seems one with the stone.)
Dinner is served; night falls; the moon appears,
a half-moon, like those circling Mother's cloche.
To one side of the potted palms, a trio
plays, has in fact been playing since we entered.
(I seem not unaware of what it plays,
of what, even then, lights dimmed, candles lit,
couples, one by one, finding their way slowly
to the dance floor, stars rising, music "means.")

My brother kicks me underneath the table;
I may begin to cry. I kick him back.
(Beneath the linen cloth, I glimpse his shoes:
so polished, so well-cared-for, so robust,
so durable, their soles so permanent,
so—what word suits them best?—impenetrable,
shoes that seem not quite his, or not yet worn,
but lent him, lent him briefly, perhaps rented.
I know my brother's shoes by heart, by heart.)
A cake is brought for Father from the kitchen;
the musicians, on cue, play Happy Birthday.
Mother and Father rise to dance; we giggle.
Through the main course, I hear the surf, now muffled,
repeat, over and over, the same question,
offer, over and over, the same answer,
neither of which a child of four deciphers,
though, in time, with such mastery as promised,
such gifts of understanding, of control,
such fluency, such vision, such command,
I may be able to have pieced together
some underlying principle pertaining
to questions and to answers, objects, words,
to one thing and another, separating
my brother from his shoes, dreaming from dying,
box from pure puzzle, puzzle from pure box,
nightingale from pine bough, goldfish from stream,
the border between paradise and China
(or provinces of each which lie between),
that faint line (tide? waves? salt? horizon? boardwalk?),
indistinct in the dark from window tables
facing the night sea, rumored to divide them.

At the Station

In a coat of the lustrous skins of seals,
a coat which floods her wrists and swamps her ankles,
sweeping the darkened stairs as she descends,
a coat which seems to fit her as her life fits,

barely, inadvertently, not at all,
her hair undone here, streaming, agitation
working across her face, each leg, each arm,
seemingly independent of the other,

tears on her cheeks now, wounds where there were eyes,
Mother is rushing past me at the station,
forcing her way through knots of passengers
assembled, waiting, alternately peering

into the tunnel's void in the direction
of the express, the last express, expected
momentarily, then scanning the tracks,
gleaming beautifully, splendidly congruent,

the roadbed dust-choked, littered with debris,
the place names on the signposts now obscured,
defaced, obliterated, the wind chill,
the light failed, failing, the noise deafening,

though the train itself has yet to be sighted.
Troubled, yet somehow dazzled, by her flight,
gripped by that show of daring in her, moved,
as always, in the company of need,

by singlemindedness as it proceeds,
headlong, headstrong, not readily dissuaded,
I marvel at her deftness as she skirts
the platform's very edge in her pursuit,

not once missing her footing, not once, not once
wavering on the brink above the track
(though the angle is steep, the drop extreme,
her position precarious, at best),

not once asking some likely-looking stranger
whose eyes seem not unkind, When is the train due?,
not once, not once, Are we late, or on time?,
not once, Are tickets asked for when we board?

This is the last train scheduled. Night is falling.
The sky is some atrocious shade of evening.
The weather? Call the atmosphere unsettled.
Darkness, as I have said, is falling, falling.

Those pelts of sealskin whipping in the breeze,
raking the platform's floor, she rushes past me,
resolute, haunted, spare, cheeks stained with tears,
seeing, choosing to see, nothing, no one,

intent on what she comes, comes now, to do,
station, departure, tracks, a last express,
her purpose, if she has one, known to her,
to her alone, shared neither with these strangers,

no matter how kind or unkind their eyes,
who peer into that void, and peer again,
who wait tonight for the express, commute
from here to there with one-way tickets only,

place names obscured, defaced, obliterated,
nor shared with me, unrecognized, astonished,

_____

perplexed by urgencies so self-consuming,
so rich, so fixed, so mythic, so relentless.

The train arrives, and Mother disappears,
enters a forward car, conceivably
takes her seat, with the rest, drawing her skins
about her, sensing how long some trips are,

how far some destinations, how cold darkness,
drawing them with a gesture faintly grand,
a flourish long ago considered grand
but now no more than grandiose, or foolish.

Walking the long, hard, cold, thin edge she walked,
treading with utmost care, or fear, or caution,
the angle steep, the drop extreme, extreme,
the song the track sings, end to end, hypnotic,

the division between roadbed and platform,
the border between station, dream, and life,
unambiguous once, pronounced, forbidding,
tenuous, indistinct now, disappearing,

I follow in her steps and, car by car,
search each car of this train, this last express,
hope for a glimpse, a glimpse, no more, of seal,
sumptuous, lustrous, light-struck, sheen intact,

draped (no doubt with a flourish) across shoulders,
overwhelming a lap, clutched at the collar
with a pale hand so that the throat be shielded
(how far some destinations, how cold darkness).

The doors close, and the train begins to lurch.
The wheels turn, the gears mesh, the grinding starts.
A woman with a feather in her hat,
stylish in gloves and pearls, serene, well-coiffed,

her flawless cheeks as yet unstained with tears,
her scent not desperation, should she speak
her voice not frail, or fierce, her collar not turned,
her teeth not clenched, smiles, waves as though she knows me,

knew me, remembers, knows me still, pretends to,
authors the fiction of her recognition,
this woman with a feather in her hat.
But Mother's hair had come undone, was streaming;

there were no gloves, no pearls, no thought of style;
there was no feathered hat, no waves, no smiles,
no improvisations having to do
with ceremonies of departure, no

head for distractions. There was this: that feat
of balance on the long, hard, cold, blue edge
of evening, where she walked, or where she fled
(Are we late, or on time? Are tickets asked for?),

gutted stations whose roadbeds choke with dust,
with more than dust, stations which once bore names
but, night to night now, line by line, go nameless,
weathering, desolate. There was a coat,

extravagant, voluminous, pure seal,
of which one could have said, This coat became her
as much as anything became her, more,
she who has come to take this train tonight,

is driven, nothing less, to take this train,
this last express, in the belief it travels
as far as where she dreams she is expected,
farther. Mother rides the express in darkness.

The Park Hotel, Munich, 1907

Now it will be all right. Thank you for coming,
but there was no need to have summoned you,
none whatever. I daresay there are cases
in Munich more deserving of your presence,
and of much greater interest, in the bargain,
than a middle-aged man who has blacked out.
My name is Freud, and I am from Vienna.
I became dizzy, that's the substance of it.
Oh, it has happened once or twice before,
and in this very lobby, I might add:
the glitter of these mirrors (the refractions
each gives off, rear views, side views, surfaces
placid, uneventful, yet strangely haunted;
where does illusion end, or fact begin?);
the odor of the carpet, possibly;
these palms themselves, extravagant, perverse
(oh, the exotic landfalls they evoke),
making one wish to ask: Why palms in Munich?;
presences (I do not yet know their names)
fierce enough so that consciousness quite leaves me.
The Park Hotel, in fairness, should consider
charging me for these episodes, these seizures;
I neither book their rooms, nor take my meals here,
but it is here I come to do my fainting.

The last that I remember is the porter
racing from the distant end of the lobby
(was it he summoned you? the bellboy?), shouting;

my knees gave way, I may have cried for help,
and then the lights went out, the marble floor
felt cool against my temple, I was making
progress (faltering, slow) against deep water
in a substance like darkness on a liner
bound for a port once known but since forgotten.
Within the ship bells sounded, the deck shuddered.
It was then that I woke to find you, Doctor,
slapping my cheeks, attempting to revive me,
rubbing my hands in yours to make the blood flow.
It was the same, or nearly so, the last time,
except that then it took longer to rouse me,
and it was the hotel's very own doctor
who came running from his cage off the lobby,
stationed there for emergencies like these.

A sip of water, please? Much better, thank you.
I am feeling quite fit now. My blood pressure?:
within a normal range for someone my age.
I assure you we can dispense with that
as an explanation, even in part.
There have never been problems of that nature.
My vision, though never quite good enough,
is adequate, attended by my doctor
twice each year, when my lenses must be strengthened.
The difficulty, if it can be called that,
lies elsewhere, I suspect. Physically speaking,
I am an average specimen, you might say:
an ache or two here, an impairment there,
hearing not what it once was, nor my sight,
but what one might call wholly functional,
despite these limitations which I speak of
(and those I do not bring myself to speak of).

That begins to suggest the contradiction:
in my work it is better not to speak,
never to speak, "physically," as though mind

were one hemisphere and body another,
each following its own path, as it were.
When I discount the physical as causing
this seizure you have seen played out before you
(you and half the population of Munich
assembled at the Park today, my guess is),
I have in mind the paradox of mind
causing body to do what body does,
tricking it, or deceiving it, or leading
it where it would not think to go itself,
as though the body were without a will,
without, you might say, "a mind of its own,"
succumbing to each trap that has been set.
Mind seduces, the body is seduced.

Have you a moment longer? (Did you not
say internal medicine was your field?
I asked your specialty at the beginning,
as I remember. Is that what you told me?)
Should my accident not already have
delayed you on your rounds, might you, I wonder,
care to stop for a coffee at the bar?
I have an engagement at half-past four
but, until then, I thought that we might speak.
In fact, we need not even leave the lobby,
should there be little time at your disposal:
the bar is there, look. Yes, I know this place well,
and not merely to faint in, I assure you.
Here, I shall need only to dust my trousers,
hide this tear in my coat sleeve, wipe my glasses,
straighten my collar, fix my hat. Proceed.

In deference, perhaps some explanation
is due you. Shall we take this table, Doctor?
There was no appointment which brought me here
this afternoon. Nothing demanded that

I reach the Park Hotel at three precisely:
no patient had been taken ill here; rooms
had not been booked in my name; at the bar
no one was waiting for me over coffee.
I had been walking in a distant suburb
of the city when, standing at the curb,
standing as though it were not Herr Freud standing,
I hailed a carriage, heard myself, once seated,
give the words to the driver, Park Hotel,
nearly failing to recognize the voice,
settled back on the leather seat, then waited,
the seat cold to the touch, the perspiration
gathering on my brow, staining my shirt,
though the afternoon was as much mid-winter
two hours ago as it is now, remember,
and the wind in the lindens just as shrill.
The doorman greeted me at the hotel
(he has known me for years); I paid the driver,
he tipped his hat, bade me Good Day, drove off.
The sound of horses' hooves rang on the cobbles.
When I entered the lobby the quartet
was already launched on that tune by Strauss,
that tune deserving volumes in itself,
some innocuous waltz that melts the heart
whenever it is played, the quartet's theme,
its signature, played when it starts, at three,
played when it is concluding, after midnight,
the first tune of its long day and the last;
innocuous, yes, and yet filled with longing.
It was then, only then, I understood
why I had come, what had driven me here:
to reclaim the past, or as much of it
as I might lay hold of in one fierce grasp.

I had a friend who stayed at this hotel
(but this was long ago, you understand);

he would come from Berlin, I from Vienna
(Munich seemed equidistant to both cities),
to take long walks, have time together, talk.
He had come to my lectures in Vienna
(a gifted young man, sensitive, perceptive,
articulate, intuitive; yes, gifted);
the two of us became colleagues and friends.
Never was I as close to anyone
as I was to Wilhelm, I tell you, never.
(I should mention I am a man, long married,
who has been drawn, hopelessly drawn, and often,
to women other than my wife, my Martha,
a man with children, suffering no shortage—
I ask that you not hear bravado in this—,
none whatever, of intimates, of friends.)
Professionally, each of us assisted
the other; it was not as though it were
an echo of my voice I heard, but rather
as though I found myself in a vast chamber,
a chamber in which, perhaps for the first time,
I was able to hear myself distinctly,
the sound my voice makes, texture, timbre, pitch.
Emotionally, there has never been
a man for whom I have felt quite this deeply.
(I tell you this, of course, in confidence;
allow me, if you will, to entertain,
at least a little longer, the idea,
extravagant as it may very well be,
that, as a young man, you may still be open
to possibility, to variation
in human life, to some remnant of music,
if you will, to those things, as one grows older,
one seems eager to close off in oneself,
almost as though one struggled to ward off
too vigorous an onslaught by those forces
which would keep us accessible to feeling,

to passion, to the poetry in us,
all things unprecedented, unexpected.
And without that conviction, Doctor, without
that belief in the possible, what are we?)

I believe my colleague felt what I felt;
time we would spend together was like time
spent nowhere else, with no one else; letters
filled the gaps between visits, he to Munich,
I to Berlin, letters quite as intense,
possibly more so, as our times together.
I am a shy man, Doctor, this in spite
of all I bring myself, today, to tell you,
notably with those for whom I care deeply.
(Strangers, as you see, are another matter;
I can, for some reason, divulge the most
intimate facts about myself to someone
whom I have never seen and have, no doubt,
not one chance in ten of seeing again.)
We understood what we felt for each other.
When I say understood I mean accepted;
understanding, knowledge of the dynamics
of the changes working in us, both singly
and together, required objectivity,
a readiness to delve, to analyze,
to examine as scientists examine,
given, happily, neither of us, Doctor.
Later, of course, we might weigh what we felt,
name and define the madness we had passed through,
the passion, if you like (they are the same);
later, perhaps, we might evaluate
how we had each been changed, or moved, or scarred,
how (at least one of us) we were left haunted,
made better, deeper, caused to comprehend
(and from a vantage intimate, firsthand)
what others, ill, confused, at some far edge,

some extreme quite impossible to name,
the ones perhaps less able to wait out
what must, at any cost, be waited out,
suffer, suffer with us, the so-called well ones.

We were much too absorbed by what we felt
to hold it to the light, study its patterns,
identify the nature of its markings.
It was enough to feel and not to name,
though, from my viewpoint, names, the names of things,
bear an importance out of all proportion
to the three or four syllables they dwell in,
much in the way an overripe Strauss waltz,
despite the obviousness of the tune,
the crudeness of its efforts at seduction,
the simplemindedness of its appeal
(how blatantly it begs you Love me, Love me),
has the power, I swear, to stop the heart
as one enters the lobby and the flutist
begins those trills which lead inevitably
to the body of the piece, that motif
tender and passionate at once, the reason
you have come and the reason you remain:
this is the past you would reclaim, the past
you would entreat to stop the heart, the past.
This is the past whose anguish you take to you.
You understand that if your life should end
this instant, it shall have been quite enough,
enough that this waltz has been played once more,
that you remember what it is you suffered
when, years ago, the quartet at the Park
played away as meltingly as today,
launched on this very waltz, you and your colleague
strolling arm in arm through the mirrored lobby
(rear views and side views, views past and views future)
to the beat Herr Strauss seems to have transfused
directly to the music, intercessions

neither sought nor permitted, the raw wound
staining his wrist pressed fiercely to the notes
over and over, reddening the score.

Dusk in the square tells me it has grown late.
I like these tables nestled at the window;
they are completely private, yet they offer
glimpses, almost a camera view, of life
as some see fit to live it in the street.
My friend and I always took coffee here,
always, in fact, occupied this same table
so that we might see dusk suffuse the street,
feel lateness falling on us, thick and slow,
not needing once to look at our timepieces
to read the hour, to tell us when to go.
Is it nearly time for you to be off?
There is only a bit more to be told,
if you have the patience. Another coffee?
How kind of you to listen this intently.
Friedrich, two more coffees here, if you please.
(I trust this long recital here today
seems more than self-indulgence on my part,
that the burden so suddenly thrust on you
seems neither arbitrary nor excessive.
Possibly knowing you are a physician,
knowing, too, that you are quite young, helps me
speak in so frank, so personal, a manner.)
Perhaps it is enough for me to tell you
the bond between us was abruptly ruptured,
though the cause, or the causes, may not be
clear to me even now, may, in truth, lie
deep in the unconscious, as I suspect.
Wilhelm confided his belief to others,
his wife, a friend, that I plotted to kill him.
It was to be on one of our long walks,
the story went, as I remember: Wilhelm
would be placed on the side facing the cliff

27

(I would see to that), and Freud, Freud, beast, monster,
would quite cleverly manage to maneuver
Wilhelm in an appropriate position
(poor Fliess, poor Fliess: victim, quite acquiescent)
from which Freud, dear Freud, friend Freud, might proceed to
push him from the most likely precipice.
If one were to ask why, he would have answered:
Freud is consumed with jealousy of me,
consumed, has always been, forever will be.
If it were not so tragic, I would laugh,
I would attempt to laugh. Proper response
to such rantings, of course, would have been futile:
can one confirm or deny the absurd?

But the episode proved a great blow to me.
The break between us was something to which
I have never become quite reconciled
(and hope never to become reconciled,
an analyst might tell me, had I not
many times, in reviewing the whole sequence
of events, told myself, over and over,
till the sound of it deafened me, the same thing).
And I assure you, Doctor, you are speaking
to an authority on very few things
but (you must not think this immodest of me)
to an expert on reconciliation,
accommodations which one makes to fact
(or fails to), how we live with what we know.

This, as I said, was long ago. Since then,
these little fainting spells occur whenever,
thinking back to that time, dreaming the dream
that once more we are close, exchanging visits,
writing the most impassioned letters, mind you
(even now, even now, I feel love for him),
I pass the Park Hotel (more accurately,
find excuses to pass the Park Hotel),

enter the lobby, greeted by the doorman,
trade Good Days with the porter, with the bellboy,
cross on the carpet, glance first to the stairs
(young girls scrubbing the marble till it glows),
then to the slender cage housing the lift,
all sensuous curves and filigree plumes,
peer even past the pastel-tinted palms,
strategically deployed (meant to restore
something of the exotic to our lives,
something, this far north, we may have forgotten),
as though somehow I thought my friend, my colleague,
now, or presently, were, in fact, descending,
Wilhelm himself, to the lobby to meet me,
immaculately tailored, fresh starched shirtfront,
shoes fairly gleaming, beard trimmed, smile in place,
the musicians beginning to strike up
(it is always three, as I envision it)
the same Strauss theme, mindless to an extreme,
the theme that broke the heart and once more breaks it.
Turning into that corridor where blindness
is the thing to be risked just where we turn,
rear views and side views, views holding a past,
summing a present, portending a future,
I can feel myself shudder as those mirrors
show me to myself, give back the reflection
of who I was, what I felt, to what end,
all much too late, too lost, to be retrieved.
Impaled on those refractions, I grow dizzy:
is that Wilhelm, my own Wilhelm, descending
to meet me, hand gripping the banister,
or a tourist departing, looking past me
to the porter, raising an arm to signal
his wish that a carriage be hailed at once,
a tourist with a beard, of course, his shirtfront
freshly starched, his shoes gleaming, smile in place?
Wilhelm?, I cry, Wilhelm?, crossing the lobby,
trembling if it is he, trembling if not,

---

not yet certain, not willing to be certain,
it is not Wilhelm, Wilhelm from Berlin,
who has come to the Park Hotel expecting,
half-expecting, hoping, to find me here,
here, after such long drought, still waiting for him,
faithful, devoted, unchanged, unimpaired,
as though nothing whatever intervened,
nothing altered between us all these years,
as though we had arranged to meet at three,
just as the quartet would be striking up,
planned that way by us, overlooking nothing,
not the slightest detail—sky, coffee, music—
we connoisseurs of least details: a table
at the window, dusk falling, thick and slow,
the winter darkness sifting to the street,
everywhere lights lit, everywhere the Park,
oh, our beloved Park, ablaze with light,
ablaze, I tell you: chandeliers, palms, marble,
the golden heads of girls who scrub the stairs,
the buttons on the waistcoat of the doorman.
I am, by now, wholly disoriented;
the Strauss, those languorous, seductive measures
filled with gestures of longing, of romance,
seems, to my ear, to sound like someone breathing,
labored, irregular, to small avail
(my infant son, gasping? my father, dying?
Wilhelm himself, calling to me, in pain?),
turns suddenly quite dissonant, quite strained,
as though nothing, nothing, can keep the music
(the heart as well, I now suspect) from breaking.

When I wake, there are faces in a circle
peering down at me, doorman, porter, bellboy,
even the tourist I mistook for Wilhelm,
poor man, looking solicitous but grim.
The marble floor feels cool against my temple.
Someone slaps both my cheeks; taking my hands,

someone (in this case, Doctor, you) is kneading,
gently but firmly, my cold hands in his.
My hat, it seems, has landed near the lift;
one shoe is scuffed, my glasses are not shattered,
though my spill has sent them across the lobby;
my trouser knees are dusty, and my frockcoat
shows a small tear, see here?, on the right sleeve
which, when I am safely back in Vienna,
Martha will scrutinize, you may be certain,
shrugging as I offer my explanation
(rather, my attempt at an explanation;
no need to worry her unduly, is there?),
taking care that the stitches barely show
as she mends it by lamplight that same evening,
the spools and bobbins in her sewing basket
arranged precisely, color, texture, weight.
(Martha craves order. Is that, you suppose,
true of most women? Do traits have a gender?)

Otherwise, it would seem I am intact.
Which brings us, fortunately, to the present.
Do you ever have business in Vienna?
I would be happy if you came to visit.
Perhaps I have a card I can leave with you;
yes, here it is: S. Freud, Berggasse 19.
My specialty? Psychic disorders, Doctor,
and, as I said before, if half in jest,
enabling some to live with what they know.
Now I insist that you be on your way;
I know how frenzied a new practice can be.
You must forgive me if I have detained you.
I am fine, I assure you. When you leave me,
I will ask the porter to hail a carriage,
will quite enjoy the ride through darkened streets
to the little hotel where I am staying.
No, I cannot yet bring myself to stay here:
these rooms, these corridors, are heaped with ghosts.

———

31

Perhaps in time. Time softens some of us,
you know, and hardens others. Let me be,
if permitted a choice, among the soft ones.
The past? Still an abominable weight
(all that wreckage, my dear man, all the losses),
but, at last, I can look at it, speak of it;
I, too, must come to live with what I know.
These fainting spells are not quite evidence
of my success, though, are they? I will learn.
I am not slow, I am not unreceptive,
rigid, or fixed, none of these, and I have
astonishment on my side for the journey
into the still-uncharted. I will learn.
But I am deeply moved by your concern.
Now you must go. Thank you. Your kindness will be
much the best souvenir of Munich this time.
And you must think of coming to Vienna.
That would afford me pleasure. Martha, too.
Goodbye, and, once more, know that I am grateful.
See how steady I am? No need to worry.
Yes, I assure you, it will be all right now.

Sackets Harbor, 1866

Here, let me take your things. How cold your hands are;
the rest of you, I daresay, must be frozen.
I've built the fire to last as long as we last,
and I forewarn you there is talk in me
to last the afternoon and into evening.
Poppa's room has a fine view of the lake.
It's to the front, at the head of the stairs,
while mine is to the rear, facing the marshes.
Perhaps I failed to show it to you last time.
We can go up to see it if you like,
but I've put on a pot of tea to brew.
I thought we'd warm to that on such a cold day.
We can see the house later, and the view:
"all the way to Canada and beyond,"
the boy who cuts the trees for Poppa calls it.
How good of you to come, and in such weather.
Winter can be quite harsh here, but I must say
I mind the weather much less than I once did,
oh, not nearly as much, and I am thankful.
Nothing, when I was younger, kept me warm,
not the coat with the mouton sleeves and collar,
not the long scarf, not sweater worn on sweater,
not even, nights, the goosedown cover, nothing.
Poppa says the cold is our element.
Attitude, he says, is what keeps us warm
(or fails, he might have said, to keep us warm).
It may be I no longer dwell on it,
the cold, that is. It seems part of the days here,
part of the life we live here at the lake.

(Of course, this is no ordinary lake;
the boy who cuts the trees calls it a sea,
which I suppose is apt. Look at the map:
does Lake Ontario look like a lake,
or does it seem forces have worked their way,
glacier, or salt, perhaps a form of anguish,
so far inland it seems we come to cling
to the edge of something quite oceanic?)
Now I offer it no resistance, none,
and no longer do I do battle with it.
It could be said I hope for less, as well.
The boy who cuts the trees says hope may be
one's resistance to the inevitable.
I think that says it fittingly, don't you?

The day that Mr. Lincoln died, I thought
nothing in our lives would be quite the same,
nothing could be restored to what it was.
But the peaches were as immense that summer
as the previous summer; pears and apples
ripened the week they ripen every autumn,
and the lake froze the eighteenth of November
as it has each year since I was a child.
Letters from Owen still come once each month,
just as they did before, giving the news,
the very same news, ship, ship's crew, the weather.
And Owen is still wed to the *Charles Cooper,*
the envelopes are still marked Mexico,
the Falklands, San Francisco, Patagonia.
Mr. Lincoln's death did not change that, either,
and, I daresay, I expect nothing will.

On the coldest days—how can I explain it?—
when I set out early for Watertown,
follow the path that cuts through tall grass (I can
take you there later, too, after our tea),
the lake frozen as far as you can see,

even perhaps beyond where you can see,
a gale whipping up from the shore, the wind
hammering from all sides, thirty-foot waves
slamming across the rocks, the jetties shattered,
I feel warmed by that chaos, safe, protected,
as Poppa would say: in my element.
At the center of where I walk, or stand,
the wind drops, and the waves, almost in mid-air,
seem suspended an instant; where the grass
flattens on either side, making a path,
there was no path before, merely wild grass.
It will become quite still, yet I can hear,
as though it lay at some great distance from me,
the fury I have come through and must go through
if I am to make it to Watertown
and back by the time darkness will have fallen.

This is a lithograph of Owen's ship,
all one hundred and sixty-five feet of it.
If you squint, you can just make out the name
painted on the prow, see here?, the *Charles Cooper.*
The letters are retouched after each voyage
(salt, wind, and light eat clear through the hull's wood),
twenty-two-carat gold leaf, Owen tells me,
though when he wrote that, I wrote in response
it could be merely sixteen-carat, tarnished,
and halfway to corrosion, for my part.
Can you imagine men calling it home,
or, what is worse, wanting to call it home?
Oh, it's a handsome vessel, I agree,
riding high in the water, sails unfurled,
the decks teak, the bronze fittings highly polished,
but you must know my thoughts about the sea,
about a man choosing to live his life,
at least the better part of it, at sea.
Owen knows, too, but I can't say it matters
to the slightest degree what I may think.

And so once more this year, as I did last,
on that cold, clear, blue morning in mid-April,
when I wake to the sound of lake ice breaking
and, later, eyes closed, make a wish on candles
Poppa has arranged on the walnut cake
he will ask Mrs. Foster to bake for me,
thirty-one candles this year, thirty-one,
I will look for a letter from Cape Horn
in Owen's hand (the ship draws coal this time;
this run is the longest run of them all,
from Philadelphia to San Francisco,
as well as the most treacherous, I might add,
rounding the tip of South America),
in which he sends his birthday greetings to me,
then, in a postscript which it takes from one
April to another for me to phrase
properly, with the right inflection, though
the meaning, year to year, remains the same,
says the present voyage will be his last
or, should he have signed on for one more crossing,
next to last, "Trusting this may please you, Owen."
I know it will not likely happen that way,
but I need, each spring, to invent those words,
invent the circumstance, invent a change
in Owen, in my life, invent my life.
(The boy who cuts the trees claims my inventions
approach a richness quite beyond what Owen
gives, has given, or is able to give me.)

Poppa says I must wait, no matter how long.
Poppa has not the slightest difficulty
advising me what to do with the years.
Once a pledge has been made, nothing can break it,
and Poppa thinks we have an understanding,
Owen and I. I may have thought so once
myself, but I fear I no longer think that.
While I may not know what it is he wants,

I know quite well what Owen does not want.
Poppa, of course, knows what it is to wait
perhaps as well as anyone can know it:
Poppa turns eighty-six this year, and his side,
the men, that is, on his side, live to ninety
(but for his father, who did not reach thirty).
I know what Poppa waits for now, forgive me,
and I know, too, how, when he speaks of Owen,
he can tell me I must wait, never thinking
to ask whether I am able to wait,
or to wait longer, if I choose to wait,
have the stomach for waiting, never thinking
to ask what it is I might feel each April,
having survived another winter, having
arrived at spring with a life quite as empty,
as purposeless, as the previous spring;
like a sixteen-year-old, blowing out candles
on a cake Poppa paid someone to bake
(imagine, paid, which shows how far we've come,
or not come, we who have only each other,
little, pitifully little, as that is),
wishing, with eyes closed, what I wished last year,
and wished the year before, that Owen cared;
wishing, as though I thought wishing might do
what, year to year, the waiting has not done.

Poppa tells me I must think of the future.
(Poor Mr. Lincoln: thinking of the future
never quite swayed the bullet from its course
nor kept the drama at Ford's from unfolding.)
When he is gone, he says, there will be nothing
in my life but a vacant house to care for,
a view of Lake Ontario to one side
and a view of the marshes to the other.
What he means, I suspect, is that I will have
no one to cook for, no one to bring meals to.
When Poppa says "care for," I think he means

37

serve, or keep house for. Other definitions
of caring, caring for, may be lost on him,
though, of course, I attach no blame: his childhood
was a difficult one, brought to an end
when his father died and he, as the eldest,
left school to save this house and work these orchards.
Poppa's future was always land and labor.
The boy who cuts the trees speaks of the future
as though it were an avenue extending
from the present, majestic, broad, tree-lined,
carriages passing under the high arches
formed by lindens and sycamores above us,
light through the leaves striking the horse's flanks,
so that we see how beautiful its coat is,
catching in the ribs of the wheel spokes, dappling
the faces of the fares who board the coach
at some point down the line, young couples, mostly,
arms linked, holding hands, traveling together
(where will not matter, since they go together).
But he is young, twenty-one next September:
he can make what he chooses of his life;
the future seems both limitless and splendid.
He speaks of settling in the Minnesota
Territories, the earth there black and fertile,
or pushing all the way to California,
where, on the slopes of valleys, he has heard,
rises always struck by the sun, grow grapes
as fine, they claim, as any from Bordeaux.
He need not wait for letters from Cape Horn
which, when they come, will speak of everything,
the ship, the crew, the weather, save ourselves.
He need not listen daily to the tune
Poppa perfects and croons: the future, wait,
time made abstract by Poppa, not here, now.
He need not climb the stairs at night and hear
the small sounds his breath makes in a small bed
in a cold room with a view of the marshes,

sounds the size of the life one is reduced to
in this house, winter, 1866,
on the shore of this lake, in New York State,
Canada on one side, sky on the other,
ice for the portion that may lie between.

Owen describes the wrecks of those square-riggers
caught in the coves and inlets of the Falklands,
abandoned by their crews because of straits
much too treacherous to negotiate
(the tide too early, or too late, the day
too bright, if it was day, the night too dark);
the winds have scrambled vessels on the rocks,
the surf smashes the mainsails, the gales lash
the jibs, the beams, or what is left of them,
and the sun bleaches all that lies beneath it:
teak decks crumble to powder, sails to dust.
A smell half rot, half rust, hangs in the air.
The crews call it the graveyard, and the ships
making the long run past the Horn the ghost fleet.
Owen states no one aboard can foretell
when the *Charles Cooper* may ground on those shoals,
when the planking beneath them may give way
and the South Atlantic undo them all,
though, in fact, I think he might welcome that.
Owen, I can tell you, likes to be tested,
prefers, it seems, unlikely situations
in which he can be brought to confront danger,
and, ideally, in as God-forsaken
a locale as possible, like the Falklands.
Imagine, winds so fierce, and latitudes
so extreme, nothing grows there, nothing can grow,
an archipelago quite wholly treeless.
Life at the lake is much too peaceful for him.
If there is anything Owen feels love for,
it may be risk, the idea of risk.
The boy who cuts the trees (oh, how unhappy

he would be could he hear me call him that)
says that the single risk worth the name risk
is the thing that passes between two people,
both the thing given and the need to give it,
that the risks Owen takes, at sea, those risks
Owen, through the years, occupies himself with,
are the risks of a man with little taste
or talent for a life with others, risks
sought by men who find, in time, there is nothing
they can love, find they are not able to love,
who care too little or care not at all.
For a boy who, I daresay, has not ventured
farther than ten or twelve miles from this lakefront,
I do not know how, at twenty-one years,
he can have learned so much, or felt so keenly.
And yet Owen is a man who has traveled
thousands of miles from home, many times that,
but the weight and substance of what he knows
(I do not mean practical knowledge: rainfall
in remote regions, weather, stars, the tides),
what the man understands, is, indeed, meager.

Forgive me, chattering away so, putting
an undue burden on you, I expect,
with my ramblings, all the while quite forgetting
the cup of tea I promised when you came.
Please do excuse such thoughtlessness. Your visit,
and in such weather, mind you, is a tonic;
it seems I hardly know where to begin
before the hour has passed and you must leave.
And visitors are so infrequent now,
at least until late April, words must keep
until the weather breaks, and when it breaks
my silence of these months seems to break with it.
How grateful I am you could come today.
Perhaps in spring I can return your visit,
but with Poppa to care for, with the trees

to nurse through winter, and this house to manage,
time, I confess, seems to slip away from me
(and, to be candid with you, my life with it).
There, I have put the pot to brew again.
It will be merely minutes, you must stay.
I know you wish to start before the dark falls,
but I can have the boy who cuts the trees
walk back with you as far as the coach station.
The stage is always late on days like these.
Oh, it will be no trouble, I assure you;
he is more than pleased to do what I ask.
Yes, what a fine idea; it will give you
opportunity to become acquainted.
You can weigh for yourself if what I say
is so, or ascribe it to the mere prattling
of an old maid touched by a boy's attention.

Owen will ask about him in his letters.
I do suppose I write of him a great deal;
still, Owen quite forgets that, but for Poppa,
I have no one to speak with until spring
(when Mr. Lincoln died, whom could I grieve with?),
and, of course, the conversations with Poppa
are lectures on my need to wait for Owen.
Poppa grants he is bright, and a hard worker,
highly ambitious, too, but Poppa tells me
I pay him too much mind, I make him think
he and I are equals, or one day might be.
He is a man who works for you, says Poppa.
I have told Poppa Owen shows less kindness
than the boy does, that his feelings run deeper
than Owen's do (feelings for life, that is;
what he might feel for me I dare not guess).
Owen will be a husband, Poppa says,
which, I must say, is knowledge I am lacking.
It would flatter me if Owen proved jealous,
but I quite doubt my words elicit that.

———

When I write Owen something the boy says,
Owen will answer, "When is the elopement?"
When I wrote the boy wishes to head west,
into the Minnesota Territories,
Owen answered, "Write me your new address."
And when I wrote the boy said word had come back
of earth there black and fertile, Owen wrote,
"Will there be soap enough in Minnesota
to scrub such fine, rich dirt from your four hands?"

Poppa says I must tell the boy that Owen
is to marry me after his last voyage.
"Has he told you when that may be?" I ask.
Tell him now, Poppa says, speak of plans made.
"Plans are precisely what I have not made,
what Owen," I tell Poppa, "will not make."
Poppa says, "You must wait, no matter how long."
"What have I left in me to wait with, Poppa?"
I ask. "What, in fact, is there left to wait for?"
"Think of the future," Poppa says. "What future
does a twenty-year-old boy, a tree-cutter,
offer a woman nearly thirty-one,
a woman who has land with fruit trees on it
the envy of the county and the state?"
"What future does a sailor offer, Poppa,
a man who wants only to be at sea,
who," I say, "when he writes, writes nothing, nothing,
of the two of us, only of the sea,
who, in letters, uses the name *Charles Cooper*
repeatedly, and with an intimacy
wholly wanting when he addresses me?"
"Poppa, this is who Owen is," I say.
"Who Owen is, Poppa, Owen will be."
"When he comes home, when the sea is behind him,
when you marry," Poppa says, "that will change."
"But it is not possible to wait longer,"
I say, "not possible Owen will change."

"That, too, is why you must wait," Poppa tells me,
"because the future will not stand in place
long enough, daughter, for you to predict it.
Nor can you predict what, tomorrow, Owen
will be like; that alone should give you hope."
"The boy who cuts the trees," I say, "claims hope is
one's resistance to the inevitable."
Poppa pauses, then slowly, quite distinctly,
pronounces each word, as though with much effort:
"The boy who cuts the trees is not the future."
As exhausted as Poppa now, perhaps,
not unkindly, yet not severely, I say,
"Damn the future, it is today I want."

Magic

At this evening's performance, the magician,
dressed in black, in a vest with silver buttons,
steps, with alarming deftness, from the stage
directly to the row where I am seated,

remote, obscure, unpromising, locates me
even before I comprehend location,
though I sink in my seat as he approaches,
extends a hand, a white-gloved hand, and whispers,

Would you be kind enough, please, to assist me?,
the words echoing endlessly, resounding
wall to wall in a full house, row by row,
I with no sense at all of drama, theatre,

lacking a definition of the terms
(sleight-of-hand, trick-the-eye, illusion, magic),
ignorant even of how one should stand
beneath the lights, what to do with the hands,

how to arrange the muscles of the face
that the assemblage imitate composure
as the applause intensifies, betraying
none of the doubts now ravaging the mask;

how to risk, in a theatre packed with strangers,
intimacy, exposure, should he ask
what I dream, why I came, speaks of the lost,
asks me to name those names too late to name.

Now, with the house lights up, I rise to follow,
fearful that by my breathing he may know me,
by the wounds in my eyes may recognize
in an instant, even before the act starts

(even before the audience applauds
the ropes, the scarves, the doves, wine drawn from water,
the woman sawed in half who has no heart
for spectacle, for the rich sight of blood,

who looks away and files her fingernails
all the while her employer saws and slices),
I am not the man who appears before him,
my life, magician, does not stand for me.

Behind him, I see all of him at once,
take his measure, whatever I can take,
in one long, final, fierce, conclusive glance:
hair parted in the middle, jet-black, sleek,

almost delicate feet in tiny shoes
of gleaming patent leather, highly shined;
though I cannot now see them, silver buttons
lighting each step we take to the dim stage,

though my susceptibility to language,
any language, draws my attention back
not to the chalk-white face, the vest, the feet,
but to the speech, the terms of his address,

the words gripped, perfect, dazzling, in the teeth,
Would you be kind enough, please, to assist me?,
words with delicate feet in patent leather,
words with a gloved hand stretched for you to reach.

Oh, for a vest of silk whose silver buttons
light a path to the stage, even beyond.

_____

45

Oh, for a way with terms (request, address),
echoing through a full house, through a life.

Before the act begins I fear, I fidget.
I face him, not yet knowing what comes next.
Quickly, before I move, I need to know
what kindness is, the nature of assistance.

Before the future starts I close my eyes,
feel the dark, slow my breathing, dread the now.
No rehearsal can possibly prepare us.
The woman sawed in half breaks into song.

I feel the dark more deeply, further fidget.
I face him, not yet knowing what I face.
I dream: trim black silk vests with silver buttons.
I dream: feet delicate enough to dance.

The dream, I tell myself, is apt, congruent.
We are, and this seems crucial, what we long for.
What is it the magician really whispers?
The woman sawed in half stops in mid-song.

Outside, of course, things fall, move downward, deepen.
None of it seems what it seemed when we came.
Think of the fields of darkness we go back through.
Deeper and deeper in our seats we sink.

Magic, I tell myself, is transformation.
We are conspirators in our undoing.
Still, there are weights and depths to be determined:
what kindness is, the nature of assistance.

Early Views of Rio, Passion, Night

It was, film after film, Carmen Miranda,
fruit salad on her head, or some rich stew
of rice, beans, and bananas from the Gold Coast
by way of Rio, singing with the band,

an American band booked by their agent
into Manhattan's supper clubs and night spots,
sending into spasms of raucous laughter,
each time she spoke, joked, wiggled, crossed her eyes,

the bass, the drummer, or the tenor sax
(all three at once, perhaps), with her hand gestures,
with those torrents of fractured Portuguese
she rained on them, some rainbow-spangled parrot

knowing only agitation and flutter,
preening in tiers and tiers of puffed balloon sleeves,
perched on tiny Brazilian shoes, papayas,
mangoes, pineapples, dangling from her turban.

The men had names like Juan, Fernando, Carlos,
Felipe, or Ramón, evoking more
than our plain Toms and Williams could evoke,
or could hope to evoke: they were the waiters

when the action moved to Brazil itself,
low-comic types, bumblers, who sneezed, raised eyebrows
(disbelief, torpor, glee, perhaps all three),
dropped a full tray at some strategic moment

crossing the dance floor, coming from the kitchen,
dipped a thumb in some diner's consommé,
men of whom not much was, of course, expected,
going home, each night, to their wives, twelve children,

their dark stews of rice, beans, cashews, bananas,
content with that, not knowing to want more.
Or they were dapper, fitted with mustaches
and tuxedos, powdered, perfumed, pomaded,

beneath blue spots singing their Latin hearts out
(to full-blown orchestrations on the sound track)
for the Manhattan swells crowding the bar,
the tables, at some sleek Art Deco nightclub

their set, that year, had made quite fashionable,
everyone sipping magnums of champagne,
holding goblets as goblets should be held,
moving beautifully, knowing what to say,

where to go, what smart club to take in next,
cigarette smoke coiled softly on the air,
the chorus, pretty, young, their gift for dance
unproved, at best, beginning to perspire.

Don Ameche and Alice Faye played lovers,
she heavy-lidded, passive, some blonde lizard
(domesticated) half-asleep in the sun,
lifting her voice in song, at times, if pressed to,

he nervous, apoplectic, in pursuit,
not quite winning her, fearful he might lose her.
They quarreled (early), spent the next eight reels
bickering, acting injured, making up.

Alice flew off to Rio in a huff,
staying, once there, with Carmen, an old chum

from the days they sang in the band together.
Alice, asking Carmen what she should do,

was told, invariably, to let Don wait
("cool his heels" the scriptwriters had her say),
let him come after her, on the next flight,
offer proof (roses, bracelets) of his love.

(Relentlessly, Carmen cajoled, advised:
some new move, or some next move, or some right move.
It all depended on moves one might make,
might not make, might be contemplating making.)

Alice wept, often: nothing deemed excessive,
merely slow, quiet Midwest tears filling,
forever filling, those slow, quiet, Midwestern,
technicolor-blue eyes. Between engagements

(local clubs), guavas, cassavas, on her head,
balloon sleeves fluttering, Carmen consoled her,
Rio, all the while (kept to backgrounds), glinting,
ready to break, it seemed, into pure flames.

What they labored to have you take as passion
was Don, in close-up, a full moon as backdrop,
singing a slow ballad having to do
with his, Don's, inability to sleep

since they met. Would she give her answer soon?
(One assumed that some question had been asked.)
Alice swayed in a glider on the front porch
(lilacs, wisteria, nothing exotic),

tilting her head, demure, big-boned, quite blonde.
Don moved beside her on the glider, took her
hand in his, asked to kiss her. Alice nodded.
One thought one heard the glider squeak, saw Don

49

shift his gaze, once, from Alice, peek off-camera,
caught Alice run her tongue across her teeth.
One swore the prop moon wobbled, dipped, grew brighter.
Don kissed her, quite politely, on the cheek.

It was never called Rio de Janeiro:
"Rio" had much more glamour, seemed more chic,
Rio, Rio this, Rio that, just Rio.
Fox liked it that way: quick, uncomplicated.

From the corner of an eye, in one film,
one could glimpse, all too briefly, Ipanema,
slender crescent of bleached-white sand, pristine,
untracked, untouched, glittering in the distance,

deeper into the background some Brazilians
strolling, possibly swimming, supple, dazzling,
the sight of them so luminous, so touching,
their presences so light-struck, so authentic,

uncompromised, one sensed, uncompromising,
one knew it would be they one lived with, dreamt,
after one left the theatre, theirs the lives
about which we should have been told, the Latins

(bumblers, waiters, sneezers, eyebrow-raisers,
parrots sporting balloon sleeves, heaped with salad)
one needed to know intimately, they
(glimpsed for an instant, distantly, then vanished)

who, in ways not yet known, were crucial to us.
Their inclusion, of course, was inadvertent;
Fox suffered no illusions Latins mattered:
splendor, light blindness, would not fill the Roxy.

Sugar Loaf, too, was shown, as well as Jesus
(what they wished you to see, not Ipanema),

welcoming, from his peak, debarking tourists
on white liners docked at long, tin-roofed piers,

or on the overnight flight from New York.
Later, it all depended on the dark:
what Don whispered to Alice, or might whisper,
how Carmen's latest act would be received,

how she would beat her wings, squawk, cross her eyes,
or launch into some thrilling, throbbing samba
in tiny shoes, bright fruit piled on her head,
agitation unchecked, frenzy intact,

lights going up on Guanabara Bay,
ship's lights, ship's lanterns, winking from the masts
of sloops riding at anchor on black waters
(the camera viewed this briefly, then moved on:

the fall of darkness in Brazil, whatever
its beauty, shading, depth, would not sell tickets),
the first star clusters, dense, Brazilian, rising,
a full moon, blazing orange, vast, Brazilian,

appearing, jacaranda, phlox, night bloomer,
orchid, caçacha, flamboyant, loupéna,
everything Brazilian, or half-Brazilian,
breaking into leaf, opening to darkness,

the chorus stretching legs, combing their manes,
the nightclub acts rehearsing, the magicians
arriving at the stage doors, all their magic
jammed in a small valise they carry with them,

somewhere the music starting, being struck
(somewhere, somewhere), the bass, the drums, the sax,
between spasms of laughter, tuning up,
from the interior, a thousand miles

this way or that (not shown), something Brazilian,
part chant, part roar, part flame, part five-beat samba,
raging, rising in waves, profound, relentless.
Fox knew, knew well, what had to be spliced out.

Road Construction Workers, Westerwald 1927: A Photograph by August Sander

They are laying a road here through the woods.
In the middle of a stand of old elms,
a crew of ten, two horses pulling wagons
hauling two tanks of water, a steamroller,
stops this morning to have its picture taken
in the forest just beyond Westerwald.
The men, in baggy pants and burlap work shirts,
look pleased to have been asked (though somehow puzzled)
by Herr Sander if he might take their picture,
though he has not asked for clean hands and faces.
No, stand where you are standing, please, no posing.
I want you as you are, or as you would be
if a man with a camera were not passing
and had not asked if he might interrupt you.
Just move in from both sides a bit, so that
I can fit all of you in the view finder.

A road is being laid through Westerwald.
The foreman of the crew stands right and front,
wearing a silver button in his cap
which seems to signify he is the foreman.
None of the other men's caps sport that touch.
Those at the left have formed a pyramid
on the iron caboose of the steamroller,
where they clamber and frolic in full light.
Since they are young, really no more than boys,
this touch of the circus seems quite in keeping.
Their faces shine with health and perspiration;

they smile, look fit, seem, at a moment's notice,
almost ready for some improvisation,
given the opportunity, which will have
nothing to do with roads, or with road building.
They seem not to have settled into lives
from which one knows there is no turning back.
The older men, content to hold their ground,
more serious about the roles they play,
think they have been asked to play, stand unsmiling,
their rakes and pitchforks held smartly before them,
proud of their work, their skill, remembering
no longer what it is to improvise.

To the right, where the line of elms begins,
a blond youth stands beside his bicycle,
wearing the look of having wandered in
from a field he has cut through to the outskirts
on his weekly visit to his grandparents.
Today, seeing the crew has stopped its work
because a man is standing with a camera
in the roadbed before them, taking pictures,
he leans against the bicycle and watches.
At the edge of it, he will be included
in the photograph about to be taken.
He wants them as they are, he hears the man say.
He squints, half-smiles, straightens the bicycle.
The man shall have him as he is then, too.

His grandparents look forward to his visits.
He stays for lunch and brings them news from home.
Some afternoons they take the photo album
from the closet to name those aunts and cousins
from Kiel and Danzig he has never met.
When he is about to leave, his grandmother
packs a hamper of biscuits to take back,
which he ties to the handlebars with string

54

he brings each time he comes, rolled in his shirt,
since he knows his grandmother has baked biscuits
she will insist he carry riding back.

Beside him, even shorter than the boy,
stands one of the two men bringing up water
to the rear in two fat tanks drawn by horses.
He is no doubt the oldest of the crew,
a dwarf with broad, square shoulders and a stick
used, I think, in helping the animal
distinguish right from left, or stop from start.
Water is needed later in the process
to lay the dust the stones send up when crushed.
First, the stones are pulverized into gravel,
which is the stage at which Herr Sander finds them.
You know this man is grateful to be here,
calling to the ones driving the steamroller,
scouring the dust for chunks they may have missed,
grateful to hold the harness in one hand
and the stick in the other, the sun hot
when they move from the shade the lane of elms throws,
the hours of the day filled, grateful even
(though he will not admit this) for their horseplay
each morning, in the field where they assemble,
their crude attempts to hide his stick or, crouching
behind him, pull his cap over his eyes,
pleased even to be the butt of their jokes
about his size and age, to which he answers
he has more strength than the youths half his age
and can outperform someone twice his size.

At the other edge of the picture, left,
stands the only woman in the work crew,
a woman with dark hair drawn to the back.
Her cotton dress hangs loose and has short sleeves,
trimmed at the arms and neck with what seems satin,

what draws light to it as though it were satin,
and, at the bust, a bow of the same fabric.
As she stands there, you see the first faint breeze
of this summer morning ruffle her hemline.
She is not young or shapely, but her hair,
her face, are curiously beautiful.
She wears long stockings, white, and flat black shoes
one is persuaded to call sensible,
given the nature of the ground she stands on.

You know she is a member of this road crew
by both the sense of presence she conveys
and by what the photograph shows she carries:
she does not stand apart, she does not seem
to have come late or idle to the scene,
to have happened by as the picture taking
started, like the boy with the bicycle
who watches, smiles, decides to be included;
she does not hover at the edge, she seems
no stranger to the others, she belongs here.
In her left hand, against her side, she holds
a thin book bound with dark fabric or paper,
what must be a workbook, a log, a ledger
recording, each day, progress made or not made,
sections laid and sections still to be laid,
number of drums of water hauled by wagon,
number of bales of hay brought for the horses,
the cost of asphalt, sand, equipment, labor.
Perhaps she serves, as well, as the timekeeper,
entering days and hours each has worked,
crossing a field from a small shack (unseen)
to tell them it is time for lunch, or time
for water, if they wish, in the long shade
of elms they have not cut, or time to quit,
to say a boy brings word from the contractor
that it is 3:00 and the heat too intense

to continue, that they should all go home
and report an hour early tomorrow.

The summer passes and a road is laid.
Behind the woman, glimpsed between two trees,
but not the object of Herr Sander's interest,
even escaping, one would guess, his notice,
what with this crew, this woman, close at hand,
is a valley in which the grapes are growing,
nothing more, from here, than accumulations
of light and shadow and not yet disclosed
material between, which could be anything
(the past, the future) one might need it to be.
If you do not look carefully you miss it,
or think of it as objects in the distance
bunched together (lives, houses, trees) as landscape
(and landscape, from afar, is what it is),
tentative, vague, unknowable, uncharted,
having no depth or fragrance of its own.
Even now, as he asks them not to pose,
telling them that he wants them as they are
(what can they think he means when he says that?),
moving them from both sides to fit the finder;
even as a boy, of whom we know nothing,
sits at the breakfast table with two brothers
eating bread with plum jelly, not yet knowing
he will be called from the barn by his father,
later, heat building, sun intense, and ordered
to cross the field with word from the contractor
to the woman who keeps time for the road crew;
even now, with the team on the steamroller
jockeying for position in high boots
and perspiration, music of the circus
never too distant to be heard, or half-heard,
pyramids rising on the thick, damp air;
even now, as a boy, pedaling fast

pursuing other missions, brakes to watch,
leans on his bicycle, drawn by the camera,
pausing long enough to arrange his smile,
and the old man, beside him, boasts of strength
twice that of any youth, despite his size,
grateful for the attention, the inclusion;
even now, as the woman with dark hair,
her loveliness as yet unspecified
this morning (yes, there will be time to know her,
time this afternoon to dream of that hair,
time tomorrow to look into that face
more deeply, time to learn none of it can be
specified), holds her workbook to her side,
true to the keeper in her clocks the minutes,
thinking how to account to the contractor
for time, lost time, how it is to be entered
(what name, what category) in the ledger;
even now through that haze of heat and distance
in which what may be seen is merely half-seen,
or seen by inadvertence, even now,
through the dust being raised by the road crew
slowly working its way through an old stand
of elms just beyond Westerwald, the grapes grow,
fat, purple, blond, sweet, hot, the grapes are growing.

Delfina Flores and Her Niece Modesta

Delfina Flores, named for flowers, poses
through the afternoon with the child, Modesta,
named for modesty, squirming in her lap.
Why the painter should want them to pose for him
eludes her, will, it seems, always elude her,
but she will not dwell too long on that aspect.
She does what she is told now, will attempt to
have the child do the same, or very nearly.
Santiago is beautiful, she thinks.
It is he she would paint, if she could paint,
his face and body, if she were a painter
and knew where to make a mark on the canvas,
where, in that field of absence, to begin.

How could anyone think her more than plain?,
she wonders, with these braids (too coarse, too black),
a nose and mouth not small or fine, a look
with too much of the Indian, perhaps,
and little enough of the Mexican.
The child, she thinks, is worthy of a portrait,
will be a beauty when she is fourteen.
With those eyes, with such dainty hands and feet
(Señor Rivera asked that they sit shoeless;
dressed in their Sunday church frocks, it seemed fitting
that they wear shoes, as well, but he assured them
his instincts could be trusted in such matters),
she will have any young man that she chooses.
Tía Dolores sewed these blouses for them,
hers and the child's, awoke, these last two mornings,

long before dawn, to baste the final stitches,
the appliqué embroidered at the neckline,
and have them done by the time they would sit.
Let the painter see you both at your best,
she told Delfina Flores; we must show him
those who have little still retain their pride.
It is an honor that this man, Rivera,
has you to sit for him and paints your portrait.
You will become, if you are not already,
the envy of the young girls of this village.

She thinks she would prefer, given the choice,
that Santiago, once, tell her he loves her
to the honor the sitting represents.
Santiago has never told her that,
though he has told her other things, things young men
always, so she has heard, tell those they court,
or hope to court, or dream one day of courting.
Wait, Modesta, wait for a boy to want you
who never brings himself to say he loves you.
But I expect you will know nothing of that;
with such fine hair, and with those hands and feet
as delicate as flowers, what young man
will not feel love for you, when it is time,
will not need to tell you of it himself,
the pain is so intense, so overwhelming.
Be still, Modesta; in this straight-back chair
he has posed us in, how do you expect me
to hold you in my arms if you keep twisting?
It cannot be much longer; we have been here
all afternoon, the sun has set, and Señor
Rivera seems himself ready to quit—
see the sweat on his forehead, see him squint,
see how he rubs his fingers? If, tomorrow,
you behave for the length of the whole sitting,
I will give you a toffee, cinnamon,
your favorite, or almond. Would you like that?

Tía Dolores made these blouses for us;
try not to wrinkle yours. Señor Rivera
says this picture he paints will be a mirror
where we will see our images exactly,
even these cross-stitches Tía Dolores
embroidered here in front, wanting to please us.

Here, take my chain and locket. See the light
catch in the links? See the medallion spinning
in the wind when I breathe on it, like this?
That's Our Lady of Guadeloupe, remember?,
Our Lady of the Sorrows. Every Sunday
the candle which we light we light for her.
We leave it at her feet so that she knows
we have been there and we have not forgotten.
You'll show your nieces how, when it is time;
you'll tell them not to lean into the flame
when you stand at the altar, as I tell you;
you'll hold their hand, as I hold yours, you'll touch
your candle to their candle, as I do;
you'll teach them what the words are, what they mean;
you'll sew their blouses, as our aunts sew ours.
When I was nine I asked Tía Dolores
what sorrow is, or what the sorrows are.
She took a long, deep breath before she spoke
and, when the words came, they came with such passion,
such heat, I looked to see whether her teeth
had split beneath the hammer of her answer:
Another name for Mexico, she whispered.
It seemed she'd always known how she'd respond,
known precisely what she would say, if asked,
and had been waiting only to be asked.

It may be best not to expect too much,
Tía Dolores tells me in the evening,
when she brushes my hair, or mends my skirt.
It is better not to be disappointed.

———

When I speak to her about Santiago,
what I feel for him, what I wish he felt,
she says it may be unwise to entrust
hope for one's future to another person.
God and the earth are all one can depend on,
and not always even the earth, she says.
I know how hard it is, and has been, for her;
yet, when the time comes that you understand
such things, little Modesta, when, at evening,
I let down your black hair, undo the braids,
begin slowly to brush it, I could never
bring myself to tell you what she tells me.
(Love, I might tell you, if you can; if not,
if, for some reason, feeling is closed to you,
hope in time your life opens you to that,
hope one day for the courage necessary.)

Señor Rivera has, in fact, grown weary.
The light begins to go and the wrists ache.
It may be the heat or a combination
of factors: heat, exhaustion, the toll beauty
exacts of vision, darkness slowly falling.
It may be time to stop now, to resume
tomorrow, should the family agree.
The older child (fourteen?), Delfina Flores,
has a look which wholly intrigues him, not quite
Mexican and yet not quite Indian;
Oriental, perhaps, chiseled from marble,
some great, dark marble, veined and streaked with light.
Part of her beauty, too, he thinks, must be
that she does not know she is beautiful,
thinks the reverse, in fact, and so her features
have not had time to recognize themselves,
to settle into mere self-satisfaction.
Her niece, Modesta, is, like any child
her age, two, he would guess, possibly three,
available to what the future stamps

across her face, available, no more.
All of it, all, remains to be decided
and, though conclusions are impossible
at this point, one at least can say the makings
of a woman of splendor (hands, feet, eyes)
are already in evidence, it seems.
Nothing more can be said of her than that.

Delfina Flores is another matter.
What she might have become she has become.
Her years already tell us who she is.
Nothing remains to be decided, nothing.
Oh, there will be a wedding one day, children
of her own, hair to brush at evening, births
and deaths, the rituals, time passing, nights,
labor in sun-bleached fields, but the essentials,
that on which it all lies, stands now in place.
Looking into her face, he thinks, is like
looking, for the first time, at Mexico
directly, all at once, face to full light.
Though the artist is not quite brash enough
to make such claims, he would not be displeased
if the viewer, seeing the finished portrait,
Delfina Flores and Her Niece Modesta,
might be moved to cry out one word, just one,
standing before it, one word: Mexico!,
Mexico!, with that sense of recognition
overtaking us when we know the name
of something but not how we come to know it.

The girl, Delfina Flores, at the outset
confided to him her uncertainty,
if she were painting pictures, where to start,
where, in that "field of absence," to begin,
to make one's presence known, and with what stroke.
Though, each day, he confronts the canvas, he knows
no more about the process than Delfina.

Some mornings, entering the studio,
he will not know what first move he might make
(and he thinks it shall all lie with first moves);
the canvas on the easel will assail him
with the burden of emptiness it bears,
with the depth of the silences it shrieks with,
the possibilities it opens to,
could open to, given the gift, luck, or technique
that knows what can be done with emptiness,
that understands what can be worked with silence.
Then, too, one's subject rises, if it rises,
to meet you, singles you as its accomplice,
leaps out at you, seems to insist, *insist,*
everything must be laid aside for this,
implying that this moment, this grand courtship,
if you will, this romance, this pure seduction
of painter by his subject, at first sight,
presents itself, and this intensely, once.
Returning "later" will, of course, be futile.
"Tomorrow," in this case, is unavailing.
You have only to be accessible,
now, at this moment, here, rapt, undivided,
only to learn to resist not at all,
should the moment be at hand and resistance
seems to you the most logical defense
by one who stands there silent, overwhelmed,
besieged, so taken by surprise, so taken
off guard, late, unprepared, now touched beyond
any formerly adequate, if useless,
definition of touched, made obsolete
by these two girls who, Mexican and shoeless,
sit in a straight-back chair where he has placed them,
faces to light, to what remains of light,
patient, obedient, doing as asked,
like Mexico itself ready to please
(how many hours have they been sitting?; evening
already moves down from the hills, the stars rise,

the dogs begin their barking, the wrists ache),
the one whom someone thought to name for flowers,
whom Santiago will not tell he loves
(Santiago of the dark brows and head,
whose darkness she would paint, if she could paint,
bending shirtless in fields beneath those suns
too punishing not to be Mexican),
thinking all afternoon of games, distractions,
both for herself and for her niece, Modesta
(chain and medallion, riddles, revelations
wholly lost on the child, all in a Spanish
equal to music as she hums it, croons it,
the Spanish one is born to and will die with),
so that the child be still, not lose the look
Señor Rivera claims to want, or finds,
or holds to through the afternoon; the other,
the one who has been named for modesty,
delicate even to her feet and hands,
a beauty in the making, for the moment
fascinated by the tears of Our Lady
of the Sorrows (gold leaf staining tin cheeks),
enchanted by the spinning of that figure
dangling before her from thin, beaten links,
turning slowly, slowly now, in the wind
Tía Delfina, out of tenderness,
has devised for her, turning in a way
not unlike the way the continent turns
beneath them, as they sit there (all of it,
forest, lagoon, swamp, cordillera, salt flat,
pasture, scrub, mesa), turning in the only
direction it can turn, downward to evening,
the mountains plunging fiercely to the sea
and the sea slipping underneath the mountains
where the darkness accumulates, or blindness,
or the thing, not yet named, Tía Dolores
calls Mexico, our Mexico, our sorrow.

In the Dark

Michael at New Hope, July 4

From what facts you gave, or refrained from giving,
I have not quite been able to determine
whether a porch graces the girl's aunt's house
(gingerbread cornices, filigree arches)
where, in the evening, after talk, green tea,
after the table has been cleared, the chairs
arranged, or rearranged, lamps dimmed, the stars lit,
one moves, with the others, to take the breeze
(any merest stirring of leaves suffices),
the air smelling of dusk, of moss, of woods
to the rear, or the side, of the frame house
(directions will be useless: in the dark
all falsify, mislead, are wholly suspect);
whether the upstairs windows face the river
or look out on the towpath, the canal;
whether, at a speed reckless but triumphant,
a car, just one (all that is necessary
for this vision of farewell and departure),
negotiates the turn to River Road
effortlessly, as we foresaw it would,
as though it were the route that entered dreaming
(which, in the dark of certain nights, it is).

Small matter, you may say, and yet, all night,
remembering what I may have forgotten,
darkness in all its aspects, the sheer weight
of fragrance, summer, dreaming, on the porches,

wracked by the thought of backroads, of July
in certain unnamed, moonlight-dappled counties,
the sweep of certain long views, placements, landscapes,
you with the road opening out before you
as tellingly as though it were your life
(which, on certain summer evenings, it is),
I dreamt of Roman candles you had brought,
wrapped with great care, no doubt, for the trip south,
unwrapped with at least equal care, arriving,
stunned by the arc they make, or would make, hurling
themselves against the limits of that sky,
haunted by rockets scrawling, over and over,
unmistakable omens on the air,
signs we decipher only when they vanish,
should we recall the shapes they took, descending,
jets, plumes, pinwheels, cascades, flames heaped on flames.
I pictured, too, the view the bedroom offers,
flotillas of canoes making their way
up-river, down-, their hulls threading the darkness
cross-stitch by cross-stitch, patiently, in silence,
in the moonlight their prows resplendent, gleaming,
the crews anonymous, intent, their paddles
breaking water as though water were silk,
thought it possible the girl's aunt had lace
draped at the windows, lace that billows, placed
soap in the dresser drawers that they smell sweet,
imagined that, all night, the hiss of tires
on asphalt, River Road artfully plotted
at an angle just beneath where you lie,
burdens your dreaming, or becomes your dream,
keeps you awake with all that sound implies:
voyages, backroads, farewells, embarkations.

Summer is like that this year (explanations
neither asked for nor given): in the dark,
strangers addressing strangers, and by names
only those they have lived with, loved, could know;

unaccountable vistas where the road turns,
where the prospect reveals, as one draws closer,
perspectives one has never seen before,
or perhaps half-seen, imprecisely seen,
the whole configuration startling, new,
a sudden clearing, moss, towpath, canal,
a stand of beeches poised on one embankment,
their branches reaching almost to the water,
their sense of presence luminous, pronounced,
the quality of what seems their attention
(to the wind, to the darkness, to each other)
unfaltering, relentless, undistracted,
lovely enough, one thinks, to change one's life;
on a half-landing in the girl's aunt's house,
that pause between remember and forget
on the ascent to second stories, attics,
those rooms abandoned, those closets sealed off,
their doors, inevitably, bolted, shuttered
("This section of the house need not concern us"),
a weak spot where the floorboard sags, a creak,
though one recalls no weakness here before,
a threadbare patch of stair tread, grease-soaked, streaked,
opening suddenly beneath one's feet,
though the flight was intact the night we came;
a small, dark, all-but-noticeable flaw
in the wallpaper leading to the hall,
some subtle interruption of the pattern
(gentian and cabbage roses on a trellis),
time stain, light mark, weather discoloration,
as though a picture which had hung here once,
a photograph, perhaps, of someone lost,
someone from the past, husband, brother, lover,
the eyes gone yellow, the mouth rimmed with dust,
had been removed just before one's arrival,
for reasons neither questioned nor disclosed;
at some still quite fair distance from the car,
a figure walking River Road, ahead

(it is late, and the night lies windless, calm),
wearing a hat, headed south, drenched with darkness,
turning back to look when he hears our motor,
splattered with moonlight leaking from the beeches,
someone we slow our speed for (Want a ride?)
only to lose him (river? woods? canal?),
only to find the man has disappeared;
at a table two tables from our own
in a Cuban restaurant we have entered
one night, for the first time, alone, a man,
having pondered the choices on the menu,
still undecided, visibly uncertain,
asking the waiter what he recommends,
to which the answer comes, in Cuban Spanish:
Perhaps regret over the vanished past;
on the white wicker porches, in the dark,
where we are gathered late these summer evenings
to take the breeze, to prepare, in some fashion
(the arranging of chairs, the rearranging,
the movement to positions at the rail),
for those festive nights-of-the-holiday
when fireworks are scheduled to be launched
from below us, at midnight, on the river
(jets, plumes, pinwheels, cascades, flames heaped on flames),
the children's bedtimes postponed, or forgotten,
the memory of portraits in their frames
snatched from the wall expunged, if not their stains,
a surf of voices breaking on all sides,
rolling in on the dark, beating against us,
voices addressing us as though they knew us,
human voices, pitch-perfect, pure, intense,
unrecognizable and yet familiar,
coming from all directions (though direction
does not matter, will be made not to matter),
from the right, or the left, behind, before us,
from the porch itself, or the road beyond,
from the woods, where the dark comes down so deeply,

telling us what we knew once, but forgot,
time, or the past, that what was possible
(one's life, perhaps) may yet be possible
here in the fierce, full darkness of these porches,
where we wait for the breeze, assailed by voices,
the words suffused with longing, made to carry
an intimacy words have never carried
in this county, beyond, a sense of risk
sitters in the dark on leaf-dappled porches
seem never to have risked, the most outrageous
poetry spilling from the mouths of madmen
who, just due north or west of here, a distance
no greater than the next village, appear
almost sane if one does not look too closely
(the way, some nights, they walk, then disappear
into the calm, clear dark from which they came),
does not ask what they dream of, what they long for.

Circus

My cousin worked the camera at The Strand
on the night shift, four in the afternoon
until the last showing, eleven-thirty,
of the main feature, paid dues to the union
(projectionists') each week, on lower Broadway,
had two brown chows, a white spitz, a dim flat
on a nondescript fringe of Greenwich Village
(tenements giving way to packing houses,
to freight yards, railway crossings, loading docks),
and a thin wife who favored black straw hats
with long kid gloves reaching above the elbow,
a girl who came north thirty years before,
leaving a quite genteel, Virginia girlhood
behind her when she came, and who now taught
Chopin études at the conservatory,
fed three dogs from her plate, never had children.

Just eleven, I had an invitation
from my cousin suggesting that I travel
downtown to The Strand, late one afternoon,
that I give my name to the ticket taker,
an old man wearing braid and silver buttons
festooning a red jacket piped in black,
who, following instructions, would admit me,
first, to see the movie playing that week
(Ann Sheridan, perhaps: The Strand booked Warner
Brothers films, never Fox or M.G.M.),
then proposing I make my way backstage
(my cousin would be waiting in the wings)

to view, firsthand, the workings of the theatre,
"Bill's theatre," as I called it at eleven
and as, even now, even now, I call it.
(Why I had been invited seems obscure,
but it may well have had to do with this:
my cousin and his wife never had children.)

During the war, even to ride the subway
downtown was high adventure for a boy,
eleven, poised beside the motorman
in the first car, stationed at the glass door
to peer into those tunnels, track by track,
to peer, and peer, and know no end to peering,
to feel the pull of slow acceleration,
station by station, stops looming, receding,
as the express barreled its way downtown,
the music of "Cathedral Parkway," of
"Columbus Circle," the exhilaration
of destinations, motorman, of journeys
begun, barely beginning, embarkations,
platforms rushing past, speed, anticipation,
travel in the profoundest sense of travel,
I, with a cousin waiting in the wings
who manned the camera, night shifts, at The Strand,
a boy whose name a white-haired ticket taker
knew, or would know, when it was time, whose presence,
it seemed, would not be wholly unexpected.

During the war, even to walk on Broadway
was voyage enough for a boy, eleven,
hurrying to the theatre after four,
uniforms filling main streets, side streets, cross streets,
uniforms of bell-bottoms, starched white middies,
olive drabs, that quite singular, dull green
Marines alone, it seemed, had been allotted,
girls with fresh permanents in short, tight skirts
and spike-heeled, sling-back wedgies, toes exposed,

stopping a soldier for a match, a sailor
for cigarettes, then, for the match, or asking
anyone for the time, afternoon, evening,
though the girls each wore watches and one knew
the hour hardly mattered to them, that daylight
must have seemed as glamorous, as exotic,
as suffused with the possible, as darkness,
the sun descending, the thin band of Hudson
River hammered into gold leaf, the lights
being lit, bands and combos tuning up,
a violin's F sharp, a piano's C,
the lean, tentative strains of an ensemble
rising, drifting like smoke across the air,
anticipation building, from the very
edge of the eye that glimpse, quite inadvertent,
of the spillage of evening in the distance,
leaking to the horizon deep, cold purples,
the stars, the first stars, fragile, pale, ascending,
the music starting, from the orchestra
pit the cue master giving some small sign
(nothing more than a hand raised, or not quite raised,
a change in breathing, say, a flex of wrist,
nothing more, simple, spare, almost unnoticed,
yet, when at last it came, immaculate,
unmistakable, unambiguous)
that it is time, that the white-gloved conductor,
baton poised in mid-flight, must, in a moment,
responsive to the cue, give the long downbeat
for the first, grand flourish of trumpets, drums,
opening the overture, indicating
the performance is about to begin,
the performance has already begun.

After someone sang The Star-Spangled Banner,
off-key, planted beside a lighted flag
fluttering in the breeze of an electric
fan placed offstage, not wholly out of view;

after a bear rode a small tricycle,
circled the stage on yellow roller skates,
skipped rope, jumped hoops, smoked cigarettes, ate popcorn
from the palm of his master, danced a waltz,
first alone, then hand in hand with the man
who gave commands in the gentlest of voices,
crooning, coaxing, cajoling, making certain
always to say the bear's name ("Sacha . . . Sacha . . .")
with each of the instructions he would give,
as though he might yet teach the animal,
through repetition, three toy ropes of beads,
pink beads, girdling its neck, a lace-trimmed skirt,
scallops and fringe for a hem, at its waist,
who she was, or might be, what sense of self,
of half-self, one quite patient young man ("Sacha . . .
Sacha . . .") had attempted to pass on to her;
after a man in evening clothes persuaded
wine to flow from a pitcher filled with water,
made a dove out of what had been a rabbit,
winking to those out front, as though implying
magic demanded not merely two hands
steeped to the wrists in transformation, ladies
and gentlemen, but the complicity
of an audience, waiting, hushed, expectant—
a woman in blue panties and gold pumps,
wearing a sequined hat to match her shoes,
pranced left to right across the stage, replacing
the card naming the bill we had just seen
(Little Sacha, the Bear Who Smokes and Dances)
with the card announcing what act would follow
(Mario, Roy and Constance, Aerialists,
The Grand National Circus of Brazil),
patting the easel on which the cards rested
before prancing off, right to left, saluting
(herself? the audience?) as she retreated,
shaking a small, half-bare, sequined behind.

Mario, in black tights, hoisting himself
on a rope dangling from the left trapeze,
had black curls, a small, black VanDyke, an earring
which caught glimmers of light each time he moved,
smiled often, raised an arm above his head,
bowed to the audience, smiled again, waved.
Constance, her entrance seeming more dramatic
with the long strides she took to enter, followed,
enveloped in red leotard and cape
whose hand-stitched borders sported appliqués
of jagged, velvet inserts shaped like flames
curling in from both sides where, at the center,
stood Constance, soon, it seemed, to be consumed,
her hair matching the color of her costume,
midway between crimson and conflagration,
mounting, as well, a rope to the trapeze
positioned at the right side of the stage,
her passivity striking in the face
of the fate the flame-cape would soon inflict,
seemed destined to inflict, held in its grip,
caught in its folds, as she was, her indifference
transcendent, vast, complete, her acquiescence
beautiful to behold, her boredom stunning,
if it was boredom, a small, quiet triumph
for the inscrutable in other lives,
for all (the greater part) still unexplained,
still resolutely unexplainable.

A third trapeze, between them, at stage center,
higher, much higher, than the ones which flanked it,
bathed in light from the wings as bright as moonlight,
stood empty, waiting, swaying, almost ghostly.
Seconds passed, grew to minutes; the stage darkened.
Then, from the roof, accompanied by drum rolls,
by a vague nervousness roiling the score
from which sixty musicians read intently,
rumblings in the strings, whispers, muted thunder

from the wind section, never heard before,
glissandos in the tympani more like
a long, uneasy shudder than like music,
a third figure, in a skin-tight white suit,
blindingly white, was lowered on a cable
lashed to his waist, a man with straight black hair,
a thin mustache, taller than Mario,
leaner, and somehow darker, never smiling,
with the body, so it seemed, of a dancer,
tapered feet, tapered hands, long neck, small head,
not bowing, not raising an arm, not waving,
looking neither to stage right nor stage left
on the descent, neither to Mario,
his twin, nor to Constance, Mario's wife,
staring, instead, into the audience,
into the darkness where the audience,
according to tradition, should have been,
was, onstage, rumored to be. Enter Roy.

Mario, catching Constance as she fell
from her trapeze to his, shouted her name,
cheered her, called "Bravo" to her, beat his palms,
turned to the audience and, pointing to her,
encouraged their applause, as well. The spotlight
searched the air for her, this way, that, then searched
again, finally found her, a foot first,
widened to capture all of her. As always,
Roy looked neither to Mario nor Constance
but peered into the audience, into
the darkness where the audience should be,
steeling himself (no one quite knew for what),
focusing his attention, concentrating
on the thing he would soon be called to do,
on the dark, or on stage dust, or on nothing
more momentous than the shape of his breathing,
the intervals between breaths shorter now,
the heart starting to pound, the sweat appearing.

Constance, now upside-down on her trapeze,
locking her ankles in the cross-bar, swung
lazily back and forth, and back and forth,
that waterfall of crimson, cape-matched hair
cascading downward nearly to the floor,
Roy, at the proper moment, pushing out,
soaring above the stage, leaving his perch,
dropping into the void beneath him, netless,
catching her flaming tresses in mid-flight,
a man with tapered feet and tapered hands
inch by inch, rung by rung, making his way,
difficult, solitary, in the dark,
climbing this woman's waterfall of hair,
hand over hand, fist over fist, attempting
all the while to draw closer to her, looking
not downward and not upward, looking under
no circumstance into her eyes, betraying
no emotion on his Brazilian face,
none, that is, we were able to discern,
none whatever, not indifference, not
delight, not pleasure, not displeasure, making
anything but what one might have called progress
up the treacherous, red rope of her hair,
gripping the chaos of those locks as though,
tenderly, tenderly, it was by grip,
by grip alone, he might be saved (the woman
betraying only boredom to us, sailing
languidly back and forth, back and forth), wearing
the look of someone for whom everything,
even this, or particularly this,
this flight from high trapeze to high trapeze,
this dream, each night, of hair-becoming-ladder,
this struggle on the rope, this drawing closer,
this fever of ascent, this rage for climbing,
seems implausible, too meager to speak of,
wholly, if the truth were known, without purpose,
distractions, say, in a life largely wasted.

In the wings, they dried themselves with a towel
brought to them by a stagehand, then returned
several times, apart, to take their bows.
The audience applauded, whistled, roared,
stamped its feet in approval, called for more.
Mario beamed, gestured to Roy, to Constance;
Roy stood erect, unmoved, unmoving, looking
past the faces before him, seeing nothing
(or seeming to see nothing, so one thought);
Constance bent from the waist, supremely bored.
Mario and his wife took bows together,
joining hands as they did. Mario, twice,
glanced at her, but she managed to look elsewhere,
attending, first, to straightening her hair,
then to smoothing her cape. The brothers followed,
wrapping their arms about each other's shoulders,
double-somersaulting, standing in place
until the spotlight, veering this way, that,
searching the dark, at last impaled their forms.
Backstage, they were much older than I thought,
smaller, suddenly made quite vulnerable,
greasepaint clotting the creases at their eyes,
powder caked in the folds lining their necks,
trailing the smell of opera, theatre, circus,
supple, exotic, opulent, Brazilian.
Even here, even here, pulleys and props
scattered across the stage, tightropes and trap doors
littering the bare floor, they picked their way
deftly, delicately, maneuvering
past Sacha's tricycle and yellow skates,
past wicker cages housing rabbits, doves,
pitchers of wine dreading the change to water
(or water longing to be turned to wine),
stale popcorn, one gold pump, a sequined hat,
a flag (American), a fan (electric),
the ribs and slats of a discarded easel.
My cousin introduced me (Mario

slapped my back, shook hands, said my name twice; Constance
fingered her ringlets, smoothed her cape; Roy nodded,
pretending to see nothing), and I stammered
how miraculous I had found their act,
their discipline, their timing, their precision
("beautiful" may have been one of the words
used in conveying to them my enjoyment:
at eleven, I pictured "beautiful,"
as much as I could picture anything,
as the highest good, the thing one might live for).
Mario questioned me ("What is it like
to be eleven? I hardly remember."),
asked if I could yet say I liked my life
("that seems the one essential, in New York,
in Brazil, to like the life one has chosen.
Mario likes his life, and so does Constance;
I never speak for Roy, you'll have to ask him"),
whether I wished to be "an entertainer,"
as he put it, told stories of their youth,
Roy's and Mario's, said he studied opera
as a boy in Recife, offered half
a Monteverdi aria to prove it.
When I applauded, moved, impressed, he hugged me.
Constance removed her makeup, Roy undressed.

Whether they were Brazilian hardly mattered.
Whether the dust-blown sideshow they had come from,
touring, of late, those towns not on the map,
those provinces in the back-country, nameless,
parched between seasons, parched, as well, in season,
was, as their card reported, National,
or, in any sense of it, known as Grand,
is not, then or now, easily determined.
Whether, in fact, a land mass called Brazil
lay to the south as it lay in the mind,
sweltering, vast, possible, light-drenched, foreign,
of a boy, eleven, for whom the concept,

that alone, was enough ("Brazil," "Brazil"),
was, and perhaps remains, sheer speculation.
Whether, in his youth, Mario had walked
shantytown's streets, penniless, shoeless, in the
dimmest alleys broke into Monteverdi,
on the wharves, at the seawall, on the beaches,
pitch-perfect, pure, full-throated, bold, impassioned,
his voice filling Recife like the sun,
this sweet-voiced child, this prodigy, this future
tenor whom they would ask to sign a contract,
once he had trained abroad and come back famous,
to appear at La Scala or the Met,
seemed of little consequence at eleven.
I was standing beside them, speaking to them
(Mario smiling, Constance primping, Roy
saying little, seeing nothing, undressing),
letting Brazil wash over me in waves,
late one afternoon in a dressing room
smelling of opera, theatre, circus, backstage
(one long, hazardous flight up) at The Strand,
five-shows-a-day, their act closing the bill,
The Grand National Circus of Brazil,
the future and the past irrelevant.

Whether the girl who introduced the acts,
placing, replacing, sign cards on an easel
not yet battered and warped, not yet discarded,
placards announcing which act would come next,
a girl perhaps from Scranton dreaming one dream,
with the rest of us (Broadway, Broadway), wearing
blue panties, sequined hat, and pumps of gold,
would find herself, years later, on Fourteenth Street,
remembering the steps she took, the steps
she did not take, that choreography
of entering and leaving, blurred, misplaced,
telling fortunes behind a beaded curtain
meant to shade the sun's glare, soften the light

(her eyes see not as clearly what they saw,
tears seem to fill them, she no longer dreams),
where it hammers the window of the storefront
above which she now rents a room and, evenings,
heats a weak broth of carrot tops and onions
on an improvised hot plate with one burner,
could not have been foretold then by a boy
speeding downtown one afternoon (Cathedral
Parkway, Columbus Circle), the express
running on schedule, beautifully, invited
by a cousin with two brown chows, a white spitz,
a cultured wife (gloved, hatted), and no children.

And if a man, once young, cries out in sleep
the name of someone, something, once familiar
(mere stray fragment, mere half-forgotten remnant),
a name perhaps once dearer than all others
("Sacha, come here. Sacha, don't be afraid"),
the men with weathered faces on the cots
lining the stalls beside him in the shelter
(Home for Indigent Single Men, the sign reads)
nod, mumble "It's a dream," turn back to sleep,
believing it must be a wife, a child,
now lost, of whom he dreams, whom he addresses
in broken dream-speech, jumbled, garbled, slurred,
though they know, too, each of them, it is late,
too late, to dream of anyone, too late
to hope to gather some small strength sufficient
to find (once more, once more, just once) the terms
of adequate address, just once the terms
of intimate address, within oneself,
just once, embracing, selfless, fierce, too late
to shape the words, word by word, on the lips
and not, mid-sentence, falter, hesitate
over pronunciation, over meaning,
nicknames, endearments, language that caresses,
too late to do more than drift back to sleep

or lie awake waiting for dawn to break
over the line that snakes its way to breakfast
(Wait Your Turn, Take No More Than You Can Eat),
coffee, fried egg, where men with weathered, once
unbelievably patient faces ("Sacha . . .
Sacha . . ."), lovely for all one might have read once
into them, men for whom, with the rest of us,
it is, or always was, late, too late, wait,
dreaming, those who persist in dreaming, dreams
(Form A Line, Dream No More Than You Can Dream)
of opera, or of theatre, or of circus.

The Model in the Deep Blue Limousine

This shade may be called midnight, but the light
hurts the eyes with the shimmer of refractions,
it is summer, late morning, and the day,
beyond the car, breaks infinite, clear, shining.

From the look and smell of Italian leather
lining the roof and walls where she is seated,
in the gleam of accessories, attachments,
handles of doors, frames for rear and side windows,

one knows, despite one's ignorance in matters
being broached here, this car is not a car
to be driven through landscapes such as these,
but a vehicle dreamt, or at least rented.

Of models, too, one might say: they are like that,
despite the lapses looming in one's knowledge
(implying one can know them by their bones,
by their mouths, vaguely sullen, by those poses

never-smiling, the other models smiling),
able to stare that stare of pure composure
and not once look away, or flinch, or falter,
despite the heat which settles here, the glare,

able to seem (the task must lie with seeming)
fixed in the grip of an unnamed possession
(extravagantly beautiful, relentless)
nothing less, but much more, than self-possession.

Her jacket lies folded neatly beside her,
blindingly white, matching her crisp, pressed skirt.
Her blouse, sea-blue, is buttoned to the neck,
sports a white collar, has long sleeves, befitting

a woman being driven to her office.
The face and hands seem tanned, well-tanned (cosmetics?,
a life apart from this?, a weekend beach-house?);
light from the street impales those still, green eyes.

It is summer, the heat builds, chrome and leather
have effectively sealed out the bleached city
raging past the car, the small clamor life makes,
so that her concentration, rapt, serene,

can be directed wholly, as before,
to pose, to look, to turn, to the suggestions
made, soon to be made, by which she becomes
whatever they most wish her to become.

She is holding, in one hand, a gold pen;
in the other, the pages of a letter,
typewritten, one assumes she has been reading,
though, for the moment, she is interrupted,

turns to the street, to what shall seem the street,
to determine the cause of the small clamor
they would have you believe is taking place there,
its pitch unclear, its passion undisclosed,

a device used by the men who direct her,
deployed in groups flanking the limousine,
so that she look, full-face, into the camera,
buttoned, long-sleeved, well-tanned, possessed, possessed.

It is not, one surmises, a love letter:
how could a woman hold in dazzling hands,

riding in a car the color of midnight,
being chauffeured through streets each named Success,

whatever route the limousine may take,
a letter which commits itself to passion,
shot through and through with the intensest music,
and not once give some sign she may be shaken?

How could she not betray the least excitement?
How could she be so readily distracted,
peering into the street, if Dearest, Dearest,
were, page by page, the word which met her gaze,

if it were Come, Come now, the letter begged?
How could she lift her eyes, or turn away,
whatever the commotion at the curb,
or not yet sense her breathing coming faster,

not, helpless, feel her blood assail her cheek,
not have the perspiration flay both palms,
if it said What I am I am for you,
sang out, at last, I want you in my life?

It is business, then, she attends to, poring
long into a sweltering afternoon,
like a philosopher, into the meaning,
the deeper meaning, of words like "career,"

"the future," as the plot seems to suggest,
long-sleeved, white-suited, pen in hand, prepared
to make notation here, notation there,
to amend this document, to correct it,

make it seem somehow better than before,
intent, but for some clamor in the street,
on the letter she reads, which, more and more,
will have nothing to do with what to live for,

with summer, blindness, driving, dreaming, longing,
but will seem, late one flawless August morning,
heat building, building, page by well-typed page,
to address itself to the task of seeming.

Once, in a lovely swimwear ad, I saw her
posed with a group of smiling bathing beauties
(she alone does not smile), beautifully tousled,
sleepy-eyed, having just emerged from mythic

waters, as the scenario would have it,
raising her arms to towel-dry her hair,
a soft and dreamy languor to her stance,
her mouth wearing the same look, vaguely sullen,

outside, beyond the beach-house, sunlight pouring,
mercilessly, drenching what lies beneath it,
the sea visible, blinding, a white beach,
an ocean wind raking the weathered floor,

salt streaming from the jambs, the cracks, pure salt,
beads of water glistening on her arms,
the towel damp, real, the possible
glinting on the horizon, where the surf breaks,

heat building, summer opening before us,
the coast ablaze, the littoral in flames.
One knows, at certain moments, where one's life lies,
who one is, who one was from the beginning.

Now she is being whisked uptown, or down,
in a limousine, polished, rented, blue,
whose driver, should there be one, stays unseen,
buttoned, long-sleeved, long-silent, sleek, serene,

glancing out to the curbstone, not quite glancing,
attending, chromed and leathered, to a letter

from which she seems to read, not quite attending,
heat building, the day sultry, all at once

crying Midnight, Midnight, the word escaped
before she knows that it escapes, referring
as much to the shade of the car she rides in
as to what falls, these evenings, on the beach-house.